Afterwards, she treated herself to a long, luxurious soak in the elegant, but extremely chilly, guest bath. Skipping high tea, she chose to retire to her room early in order to catch up on her reading and her sleep.

It was not until her hair was dried and combed, her knees and elbows slathered with lotion, and her feet tucked into warm, woolen slippers that she noticed the note.

It lay on top of her pillow, neatly folded, with the word 'Buckman' scrawled on the outside of the top flap. There was no envelope.

Curious, but not alarmed, Hayley reached for the slip of white parchment paper and unfolded it. At the top of the page, the initials T. H. were engraved in a great, swooping flourish.

The note was short, hand-scrawled, and read:

GO HOME

LEAVE WHAT ISN'T YOURS.

I KNOW WHAT YOU'RE ABOUT, AND YOU SHAN'T GET AWAY WITH IT.

Hayley's hands began to tremble as a voice haunted her memory. *"Whatever it is, you're* not *going to get away with it...."*

Carson's words.

Theadora's paper.

Isabelle's attitude.

Someone wanted desperately for Hayley to leave Newhaven. The only question was...

Who?

Palisades. Pure Romance.

A PALISADES CONTEMPORARY ROMANCE

FORGET·ME·NOT

SHARI MacDONALD

PALISADES

FORGET-ME-NOT
published by Palisades
a part of the Questar publishing family

© 1996 by Shari MacDonald
International Standard Book Number: 0-88070-769-0

Cover illustration by George Angelini
Cover designed by David Carlson and
Mona Weir-Daly
Edited by Gloria Kempton

Printed in the United States of America

For information:
QUESTAR PUBLISHERS, INC.
POST OFFICE BOX 1720
SISTERS, OREGON 97759

96 97 98 99 00 01 02 03 — 10 9 8 7 6 5 4 3 2 1

To my brilliant, creative, and compassionate big sister,
Debra MacDonald Peterson.
Thanks for lending me the use of your brain
when mine went on strike.
I couldn't have finished the story without you.
I love you, sis.

"For there is no friend like a sister
In calm or stormy weather;
To cheer one on the tedious way,
To fetch one if one goes astray,
To lift one if one totters down,
To strengthen whilst one stands."

Christina Rosetti, *Goblin Market*

I give the fight up: let there be an end...
I want to be forgotten even by God.

Robert Browning, *Paracelsus*

One

❧

This blessed plot, this earth, this realm, this England.
William Shakespeare, *Richard II*

Clammy palms clasped the tiny steering wheel as a husky female voice muttered, "Come on, you rattle-trap. Climb. *Climb.*"

For the umpteenth time that afternoon, the harried young driver berated herself for her pathetic choice of transportation. Unlike most American travelers, she had been undaunted by the prospect of driving the British motorcar. Self-sufficient, twenty-four-year-old Hayley Buckman prided herself on her willingness to accept any challenge, and navigating her way through a foreign countryside was no exception. The reduced rate she'd received from the "budget" travel agency hadn't hurt, either.

She'd been prepared for the right-hand drive. She'd been warned about England's spectacular — and for careless drivers even life-threatening — back roads, marked by hazardous hairpin bends, blind corners, and dangerous drops. What she *hadn't* counted on was being saddled with a gutless, dilapidated Mini whose every wheeze seemed to predict its last breath.

A lock of dark, chin-length hair, damp with perspiration, fell across her worried eyes. Hayley pushed it away and tightened her grip on the wheel, the skin over her knuckles taut and blue-white. "Come *on*, Bag of Bones. We're almost on the down-side. I know you can do it. Here we go…I *think* I can…I *think* I can…I *think* I can…." She leaned in with her shoulders, urging the battered car forward with each new "think."

Hayley pulled the gearshift back with a grind and winced at the car's pitiful shudder. "No, no…*no!*" Her cry was half-groan, half-laugh. The situation had ceased to be simply exasperating and was quickly becoming ridiculous. *Oh, please…just a little farther.* The journey from London should have taken little more than an hour; thanks to the difficult car, she'd now been on the road for two. And her destination was nowhere in sight. Could she have possibly missed the turnoff? Twice, she'd pulled to the side of the road, certain the sputtering vehicle was about to expire; each time, she'd nursed it back onto the road after giving it what she naively considered "time to rest."

Hayley frowned as the Mini continued to grind and moan. *I'm not going to stop again. Not for a little hill like this.* For the past five minutes, the road had weaved its way along a lovely, beech-lined valley. *There's no way I'll be stopped by one of the last few rises.* At least she hoped it was one of the last. The car gave a particularly violent lurch. *Then again….*

"Oh, bother!" Hayley struggled to control her temper. For years, she'd looked forward to her first trip to England…but her imagination hadn't conjured up anything like this. She'd dreamed of vast, wild fields and lush green pastures; wide-open meadows of heathland and fern; charming villages, immense castles, and regal country houses — all untouched by the changing hand of time. Not once had she pictured herself arriving alone...sweat-drenched and disheveled after two hours of fighting an ill-natured automobile.

It wasn't supposed to be like this. She sighed wistfully, thinking of the much-coveted college trip she'd been forced to miss. *London, Rochester, Canterbury, Dover....*Hayley was swept up in the sheer romance of it. For years, she'd felt in her soul a deep yearning to set foot upon the land of her parents' birth; the college summer program — and extended student holiday — had offered the perfect opportunity to make her wish come true.

Her parents had put an end to that dream quickly enough.

Hayley's stomach muscles tightened involuntarily, long-ago disappointment still making itself felt. While her family was never wealthy, neither had they noticeably struggled. That's why their decision had come as such a surprise. During her early years as an undergraduate, money hadn't been a worry...as far as Hayley had known. It was not until the planning of the much-coveted holiday that finances had become a serious issue.

Hayley had come home from classes one day fairly brimming with excitement. But after she had explained about the summer program, both senior Buckmans appeared nervous and asked for some time to think about the possibility. Two days later, they sat down with their daughter and gave her their decision. Hayley's parents had always been both generous and loving. Refusing their daughter's simple request obviously pained them deeply.

"Darling, we *know* how much this means to you," her mother said, wringing her hands. "But it simply isn't possible. The money, you know...."

Hayley couldn't believe her ears. "Mother, you've never said anything about this before!"

"Yes, I know. Your father and I —" Camilla Buckman's delicate, white brow furrowed in worry. She looked to her husband for support. "That is…we thought it best —"

"But what am I going to do?" Abruptly Hayley stood, still reeling from the shock. "I have three terms left. There's tuition, books —" She began to pace.

"It will be fine, sweetheart." Hayley's gentle father spoke unusually loudly — a sure sign of his distress. "Don't worry about school. It's just this trip.…"

Sensitive, as always, to her parents' feelings, Hayley let the subject drop…for the time being. In the weeks that followed, however, she suggested several alternatives, including raising the money herself and applying for one of several full scholarships that were available. But her parents had remained adamant. It was clear that they both regretted the pain their situation caused for Hayley, yet they remained firm in their convictions — particularly her father.

"It's for the best, Hayseed." He'd tried to cheer her by employing her childhood nickname. "England will always be there. Right now, you just concentrate on getting through your classes. Remember, there is a time and a season for everything." The words were right, but he sounded unconvinced.

Hoping to assuage her parents' obvious feelings of guilt, Hayley eventually let the painful subject drop. But she swore one day she *would* make it to England. No matter what it took.

Hayley blinked, her thoughts returning to the present. Ahead, the road finally peaked at the top of a gently sloping hill and began to descend once more. Sharing the car's sigh of relief, the petite brunette relaxed her death grip slightly and spared a glance at the countryside.

For a moment, Hayley's characteristic good humor returned. A smile lit her dark eyes as they flickered from elegant beeches to the winding road and back again. Her full, rosy lips curved upward in pleasure. This was the reason she was willing — even eager — to drive. Above her, the low-lying Chilterns stretched in a gentle arc toward Hertfordshire. Copper-skinned trees stood watchfully at the roadside, guarding her passage, while below and beyond her sight, the hamlet of Harrington's Green — and beyond it, Newhaven Manor — awaited.

The motorcar groaned and continued its winding descent into the valley. Cranking at the right-hand window to let in a breath of country air, Hayley was struck by a draught of icy spring wind.

"Brrr!" She reached hopefully for the dashboard. Making every effort to respond to her cues, the antiquated heater rattled for several seconds, then gasped and fell silent. "Figures," Hayley mumbled in disgust, her frustration returning. "Doesn't matter, anyway." She cranked the window shut. "Can't smell anything but fumes."

Noting that the road ahead broke sharply left, Hayley took a deep breath and shifted downward while hugging the road's inside curve. Despite all its other inadequacies, the Mini took turns fairly well; she navigated the corner with ease and exhaled.

Coming around the bend at thirty-two kilometers per hour, she suddenly found herself directly upon a bright red Fiat that was half-on, half-off the road. Charged by a sudden rush of adrenaline, Hayley swerved wildly to avoid the vehicle and careened across the bumpy road, missing the car by centimeters.

"Hey!" Dark eyes flashed. Hayley glared into the rearview mirror and instinctively straightened her vehicle in its proper lane. "That was too close for — Whoa!" Her heart lurched in her chest as she turned her attention back to the road ahead and a shiny gray Renault veered across her path and into a stand of trees, barely avoiding her front bumper. "Oh...*no!*" Too late, Hayley realized the horrible truth: her California-bred instincts had led her, unthinkingly, back to the right-hand lane.

Coming to a stop was the one thing the Mini could do efficiently, and Hayley had it parked under a tree within seconds. Leaving the creaky door gaping behind her, she rushed back toward the Renault. As she ran, a wave of nausea struck her at the thought of finding the driver slumped over the wheel, but her fears were soon put to rest when a tall, lanky figure began slowly unfolding itself from the vehicle.

Hayley stopped short, anticipating the tongue-lashing she was sure to receive. "Oh, are you all right? I am *so* sorry!" Her panic was clearly evident. "Please, let me help you...." She stepped forward uncertainly.

A shaggy dark head poked out of the car and the man pulled himself to a full six feet and some-odd inches of height. Tall and slim, he reminded Hayley of a grasshopper, unfolding its long, thin legs. The man glanced at the front of his car, then gave Haley a gentle smile. "No damage done, luv," he assured her graciously. "You're not the first tripper to run an Englishman off the road." Green eyes danced. "And I've no doubt you won't be the last."

Tripper? "But I'm not a —" Hayley looked down at her

wrinkled white T-shirt, battered running shoes, and loose, faded jeans. Obviously American. She broke off her defense. The assessment was close enough. Hayley glanced back up and watched the stranger amble around to survey the front of the Renault. He moved with a slow, easy assurance and, despite the possible injury to his car, seemed unhurried, even unconcerned. In fact, everything about him seemed slow, deliberate. "You're very kind."

The man shrugged absently as he studied the vehicle's position in the ditch.

Hayley glanced behind her at the Fiat. The driver was nowhere in sight. "I — was trying to avoid that car back there." She gave in to the urge to defend herself. The man ignored her and continued his appraisal. "I guess someone had engine trouble?" she offered unnecessarily.

He shrugged again and circled his car. "More likely, they're out for a stroll."

Hayley winced. "Let me guess. Tourists — er, trippers?"

Again, a twitch of the shoulders. "Or a Brit, stopping for a cuppa."

Cuppa. Hayley registered the Britishism her European-born parents had occasionally used. "Oh, please. Tea? In the middle of the road? Just like that?"

"As you say." The man disappeared under his car. "Just like that," his voice rose, muffled, from under the chassis.

Hayley eyed the car uncertainly. "Do you...need a hand?" she faltered, feeling uncharacteristically helpless.

The man's response was a series of muted grunts. Seconds later, he reemerged, black smudges further marring his dirt-encrusted work shirt and trousers. "Half a mo!" he called out and climbed back into the Renault. Hayley stepped out of the way and listened as he revved the car's engine. Wheels spun and dirt flew, but the car remained firmly entrenched in the ditch.

She threw a glance of irritation back at the Mini. "I hope you're happy," the tiny brunette grumbled, kicking a small, white stone with her toe. *As if things weren't bad enough. At this rate, I'll never get to Newhaven.* Hayley took a deep breath of the country air and sighed. Although they were out in the middle of nowhere, it was still obvious she was far from home. Things looked different. They *smelled* different. Even the sun shined impudently from a different corner of the sky, like a mutinous school child, rebelling against assigned seating.

Despite herself, Hayley had to admit it felt good to get a break from driving. Walking over to one particularly tall beech, she knelt and settled herself against its trunk, resting her head against the smooth, golden bark. After several minutes, the stranger gave up his efforts to move the Renault and let the engine die.

"Well?" Hayley eyed the man carefully as he strolled back and planted himself on the earth beside her.

"We-ell, luv, it looks like I'm at a pinch," the driver informed her cheerfully, sounding not a bit put out. "I've two wheels on and two off. The car can't get a grip. It seems I'm stuck. Unless you want to push me with your Mini?"

Hayley blinked at the car doubtfully. Following his earlier lead, she simply shrugged.

The man threw his head back and laughed. "I don't blame you a bit." Hayley imagined she should feel angry, but the enthusiastic man was too likable for that. "Don't worry. I'm

guying with you. Besides, it wouldn't do a blind bit of good."
He nodded toward the Mini. "I don't mean to intrude on your
privacy —" Hayley smiled at his pronunciation: *priv-uh-cy*, as
opposed to the American *pry-vuh-cy*. Something about it was
strangely endearing. "— But it seems I'm obliged to request the
use of your motor car."

"Of course. You'd like a ride back into London then?"
Hayley pictured the chalk hills above her and shuddered
inwardly. The Mini would never make it. Her smile trembled
nervously.

For the first time, the man met her gaze directly. In that
brief moment, Hayley realized his were eyes that saw much in a
single glance. She blinked and looked away. "Actually," his
voice held a hint of mirth, "I was thinking more along the lines
of driving the old banger myself. No offense intended, but I
suspect it may be safer — for us both."

"What? I —" Hayley stared. "I'll have you know I'm a wonderful driver. I've been driving for eight...no, nine years, and
not *once* have I had an accident...*or* a ticket. Well, okay...*one*
ticket. But that was actually more of a warning." Hayley met
his dancing eyes and her displeasure began to dissipate. She
rolled her head gently to one side, reflecting on the tension she
had begun to feel in her shoulder muscles. It *would* be wonderful to let someone else deal with her transportation problem.
"Oh, all *right*," she admitted with a tiny smile. "I stink at this.
Go ahead and drive the crummy, old car. That suits me just
fine, if you must know. I was about ready to shoot the beast
anyway. When we get back to town, I'll hire a cab — or shut-
tle, or whatever it is you have here — to take me back to
Newhaven. I don't care what it costs. It'll be worth it."

The man was already standing. "Newhaven? Why that's

splendid!" Large, work-roughened hands reached for Hayley's strong, small ones. The stranger pulled her to her feet, dragging her away from the beeches and back toward the Mini. "I've just come from Harrington's Green myself. I'll take you to the manor now and send a breakdown van for the Renault this afternoon. Don't worry, miss." He glanced at his watch. "It's five and twenty past eleven. You'll be at Newhaven by noon, safe as houses."

As she stepped in the direction of her battered car, it struck Hayley, absurdly, that it was the perfect stranger, and not she, herself, who'd had the foresight to consider — even briefly — her safety.

Two

❧

Where did you come from, baby dear?
George MacDonald, *At the Back of the North Wind*

Once she'd passed on all responsibility for the wayward motor car, Hayley sat back against the cracked vinyl to observe more closely her victim-slash-savior.

The man's height had been an obvious physical characteristic outside the vehicle; inside the Mini, it was overwhelming. As he'd climbed in, folding limb over knobby limb, Hayley had pictured clowns at a circus piling into a tiny Volkswagen. Yet the man had exhibited no signs of discomfort. After trying unsuccessfully to adjust the seat, he'd quietly resigned himself to the cramped conditions, tucking his knees under the steering wheel and starting the motor car without complaint. For its own part, the rental responded quickly enough, as if realizing it was finally in the hands of someone who knew how British automobiles were *supposed* to behave and was prepared to demand prime performance…"prime" being a relative term where the Mini was concerned.

Unruly strands of light, wavy hair fell across the stranger's high brow, and the penetrating eyes which had met Hayley's own now focused on the road ahead. His clothes were dirty and showed evidence of wear, but the style was fashionable enough, and the cut suited him. *He's a good-looking man, in a quirky sort of way.* Hayley turned her face away, embarrassed at the thought.

If the man had sensed her eyes upon him, he gave no sign of it. "I've a feeling I know who you are." His focus remained on the road. "But I'm afraid I've neglected to introduce myself. The name's Elliott. Carson Elliott."

"It's a pleasure to meet you, Mr. Elliott." Hayley turned back to him, eyebrows raised. "But who on earth could you think *I* am?"

"Miss Hayley Buckman of America." It was a statement, not a question. Mr. Elliott threw a confident look in her direction.

Oh, you.... Likable or not, cocky men always got on Hayley's nerves. She glanced at the man's clothes again. Obviously, he worked in Harrington's Green and was, no doubt, privy to the small-town gossip. *I'd like to wipe that smirk off your face....* With the tension of the day starting to wear upon her, Hayley found the temptation too much to resist. She managed to keep her face straight as she said, "Sorry. I'm afraid I'm not your woman."

Her companion looked mildly surprised. "Is that so?"

"Mm," she affirmed, staring absent-mindedly out the window.

"In that case, I beg your pardon." Carson kept his eyes on the winding road. "Then you are...?"

"Ah-h," Hayley's eyes flickered at the scenery, looking for inspiration. "Beecham." *Oh, brother.* Too late. She was stuck with it. "Melanie Beecham."

"Beecham?" He looked over her shoulder at the passing trees. "As in *beech*-am?"

Hayley glared at him, frustrated with the turn in conversation. "Yes, *Beecham*," she answered testily, then made a point of turning and ignoring him. She had meant to give *him* a hard time, not to become an easy target. She was usually better at this. *I must be tired.*

"I see." Carson stroked his chin thoughtfully as they descended further into the wooded valley. For several minutes he drove without speaking, then, "You're here on holiday, then, Miss Beecham?"

She started at the sound of his voice. "Y-yes. I am."

Strong, calloused hands turned the wheel without effort. "And what do you have planned for your stay in Europe?" His gentle country voice betrayed no traces of doubt. Perhaps the man *was* fooled.

What a bumpkin. Hardly a challenge at all.

"Miss Beecham?"

Hayley racked her brain. Where was she headed? She couldn't think. A young woman, traveling alone, with no particular itinerary.... "I don't really have any set plans. I've...been ill recently." She picked at the peeling vinyl seat.

"I'm *so* sorry."

Hayley looked at him suspiciously, but the man gave no sign of insincerity. "Oh, I'm quite well now," she said brightly. "But my father suggested that I take some time away and rest." That was good. A slow smile spread across her face. The man couldn't dispute such a story.

"Wonderful advice." Carson kept his eyes trained on the

continuously bending road. "Your father sounds very generous."

"Oh, he *is*," Hayley agreed whole-heartedly.

"That's splendid. And what does he do?"

Hayley swallowed hard. "Do?"

"Mm, yes. Do. His work?"

She considered her options. *He'd have to be wealthy, sending his daughter on a trip like this.* "Actually, he's an inventor," she lied outrageously.

"How fascinating!" The man *did* look truly fascinated. His eyebrows rose in amazement. "What has he invented?"

Of course you'd ask. "Uh...you know Velcro?" Too late, Hayley realized that an authentic Velcro princess would know if her father's product was popular in Europe.

"I've heard of it," Carson remarked dryly.

"Well, that's my dad." She nodded emphatically. "Herbert Beecham. The inventor of Velcro. He...almost called it Beechcro, but decided to name it after my mother, Velma, instead." She felt like kicking herself. *Stop it, Hayley. There's a limit to what this yokel will swallow.*

"Really?" Carson looked impressed. "Very creative."

Hayley narrowed her eyes, but he still gave every indication that he was buying the story. *Unbelievable.*

"Your dad must be fairly young," the man rattled on. "Funny, I'd have thought Velcro was much older than that. Shows how much I know."

"Yes, well...Dad's older than you might think," Hayley mumbled uncomfortably, trying to imagine how she might initiate a subject change. "It's interesting, you taking me for that

Buckman woman. Why did you, do you think?" she wondered aloud, palms sweaty.

Carson Elliott gave a characteristic shrug. "No reason, really. It's just that we're expecting her up at the manor today. She's coming to work in the gardens. Have you seen the gardens at Newhaven, Miss Beecham?"

"No-o. Not exactly," Hayley hedged. "But I've seen pictures. They're quite spectacular, aren't they?"

The man beamed. "We think so," then, with maddening timing, at last fell silent.

Hayley glanced back at his intriguing profile and waited for him to go on. Something about his tone struck her as faintly disturbing. Finally, she could stand it no more. "*We?*"

He nodded, apparently oblivious to the degree of her interest. "The credit goes to Theadora Harrington, of course. They're her gardens." Was that a hint of an edge in his voice? Hayley looked more closely; his expression was quite relaxed. He went on cheerfully. "But she's given me quite a bit of input in recent years. Mostly because of her health, I suppose. Usually, I keep to the background. Still, I admit, it's nice to hear the compliments now and then."

She blinked, not fully understanding. "Given...your input?"

"That's right." Carson nodded. "Oh, didn't I say? I should have done. I'm the head gardener at Newhaven." He ignored the widening of her eyes. "Forgive me for taking you to be Miss Buckman. It's just that we need her quite badly, and I've looked forward to her arrival."

Oh, good heavens! One hand flew to Hayley's open mouth. *Of all people...the head gardener! What have I done? Daddy always said my mouth would get me into trouble.* She could not meet his gaze. "I'm afraid, Mr. Elliott —" she stammered. Small hands clenched nervously upon the seat beside her. "That is...oh, I've been terribly, *terribly* rude! I owe you —"

"Don't worry, Miss Buckman," he interrupted with a smile. He steered the Mini expertly. "You shan't be sacked."

Hayley stared at him dumbly. "You knew all along?"

Bushy eyebrows raised. "Please. *Beechcro?* I'm English...not daft."

"What? Mr. Elliott, you were playing with me!" Her astonishment was genuine.

The big man grinned unashamedly. "That I was." He turned to her with challenge in his eyes. "As you were with me."

"But, I —" Hayley found herself slowly meeting the gardener's grin. "All right, you have me there. But what on earth? You're not at all what I expected from a Briton."

"Really? And what were you expecting?" He eyed her curiously.

"You know, cool, aloof, humorless...uh, *polite*...." She couldn't resist the playful dig.

"Ah, now, that one hurt." His voice was smooth. "An Englishman is always polite." Hayley looked at him out of the corner of one eye. He didn't appear wounded.

"Right. And an American always exercises good judgment." She laughed. "You *are* unusual for a Brit. Even *I* can tell."

Carson nodded. "True enough. Comes of having an American mother, I imagine."

"American! *Really.*" Now, she truly was amazed.

He nodded again. "And a younger brother who keeps me on my toes."

"Heavens! There are two of you?" Hayley rolled her eyes.

Carson smiled wickedly. "Oh, yes. And we *both* work in the gardens. We'll have you surrounded."

"How lovely." Hayley sounded anything but thrilled. "So how will I know my other tormentor?"

"Oh, you'll know Gabriel, all right." Carson spoke with great assurance. "You can't miss him...unless, of course, you actually *miss* him. He's often off poking around the countryside or napping under the topiary."

"And he lives with you, I gather?"

"Always has." A muscle twitched along his jaw line. "Mother died when he was eight, our father several years before that."

"I'm sorry," Hayley offered gently.

"That's kind of you to say." The large man shifted restlessly in the seat beside her. "Actually, I'd been watching over Gabe since he was a lad. Once Mother was gone, it just became a bit more...difficult."

"From big brother to father figure?"

"Something like that," he agreed. "Although, you make it sound much simpler than it was." His voice was strained. "I have to admit, Gabe's handled it much better than I. He's been hardly any trouble. Mother raised him well. It's just that...." He paused. "I suppose I wasn't quite ready to be a parent. But then, one doesn't always have a choice."

"I suppose not." Hayley had never thought of parenthood in those terms. Her eyes returned to her companion; for the first time, Carson actually looked uncomfortable.

"Sorry!" he offered brightly. "Another moment, and I'd have bent your ear in two! I'm sure there are dozens of topics we could discuss that would be more pleasant than my family problems."

"That's all right," Hayley assured him. "Why don't you tell me how the two of you ended up at Newhaven?" she asked, deliberately steering the conversation onto less threatening ground. "You're a bit out of the way, it seems. It must get lonely." Without thinking, she stole a glance at the man beside her.

"Some might feel so. I do all right."

The words were matter-of-fact. No sign of a deeper longing. *An obvious brush-off.* Hayley bit her lip, surprised at the odd twist in the pit of her stomach. *Snap out of it, girl. You've been alone way too long.* It wasn't anything like her to be drawn toward a perfect stranger, nor to feel sadness at a man's lack of interest. For two years, she hadn't once allowed herself to entertain ideas of romance. She preferred the safety of staying busy and feeling in control. But then, she'd never traveled solo to a different city — let alone country — before. One was bound to feel vulnerable in such circumstances.

But that wasn't the only factor, Hayley knew. On top of everything else, she had felt increasingly restless, even lonely, as she approached the end of her program. For the first time since she'd lost her parents, she felt herself touched by the longing for a connection with others. Obviously, the longing was deeper than she had originally realized.

"Like the Harringtons, our family has been at Newhaven for generations," Carson was saying. "Although in a very different capacity, of course. My father was head gardener, as was his father before him. If you go back a few generations, you'll find that the Elliotts once served as vicars at Newhaven Chapel. Around these parts, it once was the parson's job to tend both the gardens *and* God's sheep. But in a rare demonstration of pity, the Harrington family finally made two positions of it."

Hayley ignored the family history and pounced on the one bit of information she'd grasped. "Newhaven has its own *chapel?*"

"Of course. Hadn't you been told?" Carson looked surprised. "Tell me, what *do* you know of Newhaven Manor, Miss Buckman?"

"Well...very little, actually," she admitted reluctantly. "I learned about the estate while I was studying architecture and applied in March for next year's internship. I didn't expect to hear anything for months. But I got a response right away. There's been a bit of an emergency, I gathered?"

"Of a sort," Carson agreed. "The previous intern had to leave quite suddenly. It was the oddest thing." He shook his head and scowled. "Francine was a lovely girl...quite talented. She was scheduled to stay through the fall. But one morning Ellen went up to call her for breakfast, and she'd just off and gone." His voice sounded strained.

"Really? That *is* odd." Trails of goose bumps rose along Hayley's arms. "You don't suspect...foul play?" The words sounded ridiculous even as she spoke them.

"My word! How gothic," the man teased. Then, catching the seriousness of her gaze, he sobered. "Actually, I *did* wonder a bit at first," he confessed. "But there was a brief note left in her room — written in her own handwriting — explaining that she'd had to leave right away. Personal matters, it said, or some such rubbish." The muscles around his mouth tightened noticeably. "Then, too, her things had all been packed. It doesn't seem likely that a stranger could have sneaked in and done all that without being caught up."

Hayley eyed him curiously. "Rubbish. You don't believe it was personal matters that caused her to leave."

Carson opened his mouth as if to speak, then seemingly thought better of it, snapped his jaw shut and shrugged. After a moment of consideration, he offered, cryptically, "It just seems odd. That's all I'm saying."

Hayley felt herself shiver. "Well, it doesn't concern me, I'm sure," she said bravely. "Perhaps she had a secret boyfriend she couldn't wait to be rid of."

"Perhaps," he allowed, cheerfully enough. "I'm sure matters will be very different for you."

"Wh- what?" Hayley spun in her seat and glared at him. "Of all the —"

Carson grinned unabashedly. "Ah, now, let's not make a meal of this. You know what I meant. I'm just saying that I'm sure you won't be touched by whatever — if *anything* — our dear Francine was up to."

Our dear Francine.... Suddenly, Hayley felt strangely out of sorts.

"I can assure you," she said coldly, "that whatever — or *who*ever — your Francine was involved with is of no interest to me."

"Of course it's not," Carson agreed gamely. "Nor should it be. But I believe I know of something that *will* be," he whispered. Thick eyebrows wagged conspiratorially.

"Mr. Elliott, what can you *possibly* be talking ab —" Hayley turned away in exasperation, then, catching a glimpse of the view outside her window, broke off abruptly, her eyes and mouth open wide.

Slowly, the Mini crept over a low, stone bridge into a village that seemed plucked from an English postcard. On either side of the pothole-covered road, small children played happily and loudly upon twin rectangles of lush, green lawn. Beyond them were clusters of assorted thatched, brick and timber cottages. To the right, residents milled about several large, stone buildings, one of which was an impressive-looking pantiled affair bearing the sign Ram's Head Inn. And at Hayley's left, along the swiftly flowing Thames, stood a powerful, old watermill that appeared to be still in use.

After anticipating Britain's grass-covered meadows and heath-scattered moors, Hayley had at first been taken aback upon finding herself in one of the country's rare woodland areas. But now, suddenly, before her was the England of her dreams. Her eyes grew damp, but she regained her composure before they spilled real tears.

"So what do you think of Harrington's Green?" Carson spoke with barely-suppressed pride.

Hayley simply stared, unable to speak. Her companion nodded approvingly.

"You think *this* is something?" He squared his shoulders and stared into the distance, as if focusing on a destination Hayley could not see.

"Take a deep breat . You'll never believe what comes next."

Three

❦

To travel hopefully is a better thing than to arrive.
Robert Louis Stevenson, *El Dorado*

The tightly-knit family of brick and timbered cottages gave way to open fields as the Mini advanced slowly but steadily upon Hayley's desired destination.

Carson Elliott gave his passenger a slow, assessing glance, then offered brightly, "We're getting close. See those lot meadows up ahead? Those are separate from the estate. They were the arable fields that belonged to the community. See there, where the road splits? That's where the land was divided into three fields: West, North, and East." He indicated each with a point of his finger. "There was a time when they all were farmed regularly. They were divided in such a way that each could lay fallow every third year."

Hayley turned dark brown eyes upon the man beside her and half-listened as he rattled on about freemen, crops, and furlongs. He spoke with great assurance and his tone was friendly, but he kept his penetrating green eyes focused on the road, for which Hayley was grateful.

"I imagine that a little bit of background might help you

since, as you say, you don't know much about English manors. I suppose you don't know how they came about?" He continued on, not waiting for an answer.

Hayley tried to follow his narrative, but she could not keep her thoughts from wandering to the manner in which she had come to this incredible place. Everything had fallen together so quickly; she'd barely had time to consider the consequences of her actions. Even as a child, she'd always been one to follow a whim but always before, her parents were around to keep her from getting herself in too deep.

Hayley turned and carefully studied Carson Elliott as he cheerfully rambled on, touching upon various points of local history. He was, in fact, the first person from the estate with whom she had actually spoken. Her only contact with Theadora Harrington had been her initial application for internship and the woman's faxed response, now a smudged and crumpled wad in her pocket: "...as we are severely short-handed, it will be necessary for you to begin immediately. We will expect you on the seventeenth of May." Hayley had received warmer letters from bill collectors. As they drew nearer to the estate, her uneasiness steadily increased. Would Theadora Harrington be friendlier in person? Would Hayley, herself, be up to the job? What if they found her to be undisciplined, untalented...nothing like "our dear Francine?"

Her chauffeur continued to babble, clearly oblivious to her distracted state. "It was actually after the Saxon invasion that people first began to band together in outlying settlements like this one." Like a teacher more interested in his subject than his students, he droned relentlessly on. "Each group found that it needed a leader: someone who could organize forces in cases of war, settle local disputes, and so on. This judge, or 'lord,' soon began to collect dues and rents — and, in fact, labor — in payment for his leadership. But it was under the Norman rule that the official manorial system began."

Hayley stared out the window, her expression blank.

"The lord ultimately became *very* important."

Ya-da, ya-da, ya-da.

"He levied fines, held court, and offered a certain degree of protection. And in return, the local tenants paid their fines and worked a required number of days on his land...which wasn't easy, considering they had their own crops to tend. His power wasn't absolute, but it was quite extensive. In fact, it still is, to a lesser degree. Of course," he said authoritatively, "official feudal privileges have long been a thing of the past. But don't mention that to Theadora," he warned. "She has more than a little power around here...although as great as it is, it's still not as far-reaching as she imagines."

That got Hayley's attention. She turned in her seat. "Good grief. Surely she doesn't still try to collect taxes? Or force people to work on her land?"

"A-*ha*. So you were listening. I had begun to wonder."

"Sorry," she mumbled sheepishly, offering an apologetic smile.

"Don't be sorry. Obviously you're concerned about something. But I can assure you there's little to worry about where Theadora is concerned. She fancies herself as being quite important — which, of course, she is to some degree. Be on form; treat her with respect and proper deference — as you would any employer — and you shan't have any trouble at all, I'm sure."

Hayley looked relieved. "You'll have to excuse me. I didn't

mean to be rude. I'm just so…*absorbed* with getting to Newhaven. I'm afraid it has me a bit on edge."

"I'd noticed," Carson admitted. "Why do you think I went off on all that farming nonsense?"

Because you're socially inept? Immediately, Hayley regretted the unkind thought. Carson Elliott seemed like a very nice man. Why was she feeling so unnerved? She blinked. "I really couldn't say."

"To distract you, of course." Carson spoke as if it were obvious. "But clearly I failed. So out with it. Tell all. What's got you all in a knot? Not that nonsense about Francine, I hope? I was serious about you being quite safe."

"I'm sure you were. No, that's not it." Hayley's words were only partly true. She spoke lightly, "I'm sure what I'm feeling is very normal. I'm just a little nervous — new place, new people…a chance to make all my dreams come true or send them dashing onto the rocks of failure and despair as I destroy my entire future.…"

"Of course." The muscles on Carson's face twitched, as if working to conceal a smile. "How silly of me not to realize. The usual. But are you certain you're keeping things in perspective? Surely this opportunity isn't as important as all that?"

Long, dark lashes lowered over her eyes, shutting out the man's searching gaze. How could this stranger possibly understand?

The happy, carefree days in which her goals had been eclipsed by friendships and family ties now seemed a distant memory. For the past two years, she had concentrated solely on whatever milestone lay directly ahead: completing her degree, establishing herself in her career. The tragic chimney fire had taken her family, her home…but it hadn't swallowed up her future.

Amazingly enough, after her parents' deaths Hayley learned that Jon Buckman had left her a substantial amount of money: vastly more than she would have expected, considering the concerns about finances they had expressed two years earlier. That surprising news was the only positive development that terrible year, and she took full advantage of it, applying — and gaining acceptance — to a top-notch architectural school in Los Angeles.

It was not what she would have imagined for herself as a child. Growing up, Hayley had been passionate not about building things, but about planting things. She adored the outdoors and spent hours with her mother, digging in the dirt, tending fiery snapdragons, sweet-smelling forget-me-nots, and delicate alyssum. Like every small child, Hayley drew great delight from playing in the mud; she never outgrew her love for what her mother called "mucking about in the earth." Even as an outgoing, people-oriented teenager, she earned money not by working at the local fast-food restaurant, but by putting her "green thumb" to work in her neighbors' gardens. Hayley had always assumed she would one day become a gardener, but her parents had balked; in the end, they and her guidance counselors had convinced her to pursue a degree in business.

"You've a wonderful, bubbly personality, Hayley," her father had told her. "And a good head on your shoulders. Put them to good use, why don't you? Don't waste your life away out amongst the shrubbery. It's people that matter, girl. *People*. Remember…plants can't love you back." Hayley was disappointed, but not surprised by his response; Jon Buckman was never thrilled about his daughter's "childish interest in plants."

As a high school student, Hayley was confused by his lack of support for her passion. But after the incident involving the trip to England, she understood. Hayley adored her parents and wanted very much to please them. And so, accepting their concern about her financial future, she had given in — hoping to set their fears to rest — and selected a course of study centered around business management. Ultimately, she developed an interest in architecture but squelched any hope of attending graduate school, never mentioning to her parents the goal that seemed so unattainable. Not until after the fire did Hayley learn that her parents had had the resources after all.

It was at architectural school, while studying how to design structures to best fit into the landscape, that Hayley found herself drawn once more to the landscape itself. Shortly thereafter, she had changed her major to landscape architecture. Her senior internship was the last requirement; Hayley's dream was about to come true. If only her parents could be there to see it....

Hayley stared out at the vast green meadows that were so characteristic of England. *Surely, this opportunity isn't as important as all that?* Blast the man. Hayley had half a mind to read him the riot act. But at this point in her journey, she felt too exhausted to spar.

"Of course, you're right. I'm just being silly." Her voice seemed small, even in the tiny compartment of the car. It sounded strange to her own ears; she wasn't used to caving in — to anyone.

The Mini had been slowly creeping forward; as Hayley spoke, it suddenly stopped. She looked up in alarm. Had the blasted thing broken down for good this time?

She glanced over at her companion and found him studying her profile. Slowly, he reached across the seat, lifted one of her slim, work-roughened hands, and squeezed it gently. "No. I'm the one who's been silly." His expression was one of deep regret. "Your feelings are your own, Miss Buckman, and you're entitled to them. Don't let any fool tell you otherwise — no matter how well-meaning that fool might be."

"Thank...you," Hayley stammered awkwardly. The intensity of his gaze startled her. Hayley's thin, finely-arched eyebrows pinched together, marking her confusion. "I won't."

The man's tanned, stubbled face broke into a smile of relief. He withdrew the warmth of his hand without another word. Hayley felt it go with a twinge of regret. In the next moment, the car began to move forward once more.

As Hayley turned away to hide her confusion, her eyes were drawn to a spectacular sight. "Oh, look! A chapel!" She leaned against the door panel and pressed her face against the Mini's tiny window as they approached.

"Careful!" Carson laughed. "I wouldn't lean against that door latch. I doubt this thing is held together with anything more than rust and spit."

Hayley's eyes shone with the same warm glow reflected by the chapel's honey-golden Ham Hill stone. "It's...wonderful!" The building was not large, but Hayley was struck by its almost-human presence. After growing up in a city that had quickie marts and nondescript burger joints on nearly every corner, she found it overwhelming to discover a structure that had a personality of its own. Strong. Dignified. Humble. At the front of the church, a lantern-shaped turret rose high into the sky; at its peak, a simple cross. Low, stone walls encircled the R-shaped church, immediately surrounded by dozens of massive, ornamental grave stones.

Hayley held her breath as their car passed. Her companion seemed pleased to see her spirits much improved.

"You can worry about what lies ahead if you like, but I'm certain you'll do famously," he encouraged her. "Theadora wouldn't have chosen you if you hadn't the skill for the job."

"I would hope not," Hayley admitted, tearing her eyes away from the chapel, now receding in the distance. "But...that's just it. How can she know, really?"

"I'm sure your portfolio spoke for itself," Carson spoke with complete assurance.

"My...portfolio." Hayley stared at him, not understanding.

"Photos, notes...of your work."

"They...didn't ask for any portfolio."

"Really? How odd." Carson looked faintly surprised. "You must have made quite an impression during your interview. Theadora always asks for a portfolio."

Hayley stared at the road and chewed one thumbnail nervously.

"You...*were* at least rung up for a telephone interview?" Carson's expression shifted from mild surprise to outright shock.

"Well...no. I wasn't. After my initial application, I received a longer, much more detailed form to fill out. After I'd returned it, I got this fax." Hayley pulled the scrap of wrinkled thermal paper from her pocket. "Mrs.— Lady Harrington said you were incredibly short-handed and asked...or, actually *told* me to come right away. Is that so terribly unusual?" By this time,

Hayley had given up all efforts to put up a brave front. She knew alarm was clearly written on her face.

"Well...no, of course not." Carson waved a hand in the air as if brushing away a fly. "I'm certain it's been done before. Unusual circumstances and all. I'm sure it couldn't be helped." He looked at her nervously. "You've studied? You *did* have letters of recommendation?" Suddenly, he appeared to be struck by a terrible thought. "You *have* gardened before?"

"Don't be silly!" Hayley's nerves were frayed; she was really irritated now. "Of course I have. What do you take me for, an idiot?" Her words were defiant, but she was sure her face was still a deathly white.

"My apologies. One...can never be sure quite what the Harringtons have in mind. It can be a bit disconcerting."

Hayley licked her lips. "Well, whatever Theadora Harrington was thinking, there's nothing to be done about it. There's no turning back now."

"As you say." Carson indicated the road before them with a nod. "There's no turning back now."

Hayley turned her head and caught her breath at the sight ahead: gleaming golden stone, high-reaching pillared chimneys, lead-glazed glass, and before it all, a spectacular, living carpet woven of brilliant blues, greens, and golds.

Carson's voice sounded grim. "Welcome to Newhaven."

Four

⚜

Him whom you love, your Idiot Boy.
William Wordsworth, *The Idiot Boy*

The resting giant loomed large and proud upon the hillside, its great, darkened windows like wary eyes: watchful, unblinking.

Hayley stared back mutely, feeling like an insolent interloper but unable to tear her eyes away.

Built, like the chapel, from massive blocks of rich-toned Ham Hill stone, the high, weather-beaten walls of the manor house gleamed softly, as though they had managed to soak up each drop of weak English sunlight and were reflecting back its glory double-fold.

High above, two tall stone chimneys rose against the sky, their more modern brick extensions looking self-consciously out of place. Between the stacks, a single gable jutted out from the steeply-pitched roof, its mullioned windows returning the glare of the sun. Looking up at the imposing structure, Hayley could not decide which it resembled more: palace or prison.

She turned away, having given the manor her first attention, as its due, and basked in her first glimpse of the crowning glory that had brought her to Newhaven.

Stretching from the house to the main road nearly two kilometers back, and bordered on the east and west by two rows of neatly-clipped yews, lay a vast floral parterre: bed after bed of soft periwinkle blue, marked by deep, rich red blossoms and cheerful yellow buds. Surrounding all were short, trim box herb hedges and paths of smooth white cobbled stone.

Rocks crunched under the Mini's tires as they traced the main approach along a line of yews. Despite the spring chill, Hayley rolled open her window and breathed deeply of the glorious fragrance. Her eyes swept appreciatively over the sea of color.

"Tulips, of course, and primulas. How lovely! But what's the blue? Oh, *do* slow down. I can't see. You're going too fast...."

"'What's the blue?' And you call yourself a gardener?"

"Don't laugh at me! It's *your* fault. Would you just — Oh!" As he decreased their speed, "Forget-me-nots! My *favorite*. How wonderful!" A feeling — old and familiar — stirred deep inside, making Hayley's fingers tingle with the desire to "muck about in the earth."

"You'll see a lot of them here, I dare say. They're a staple of the English garden, you know, and found quite often in herbaceous borders. Of course, they survive the cold of winter so well — Hullo!"

Brakes caught and gravel flew as a slight figure hurled itself across the Mini's path. Carson threw out one arm between Hayley and the windshield, catching her right above the collarbone before she could be thrown against the dashboard.

"Oof!" Hayley bounced off his arm and fell back against the seat as the Mini jerked to an abrupt halt.

"Are you all right?" All light-heartedness gone, Carson turned his full attention upon her, his concern clearly evident.

"Yes, I —" Hayley began. She stopped to catch her breath.

Carson's eyes flickered across her face, then flew back to the road. "Gabriel!" he roared. The country voice was no longer gentle.

"I say, Cars!" Laughing emerald eyes peered in the window. "Back so soon? And where'd you get the — Oh, hullo!" It didn't seem possible, but the grin actually widened. "Sorry. I didn't realize my brother had found a new friend."

"*Really*, Gabriel. She's not a stray puppy!" Carson tried to sound fierce, but the tone was unmistakably forced. "And what in heaven's name do you think you're doing, flinging yourself across the road like that? You're lucky I didn't flatten you."

"Oh, no...*you're* lucky!" the boy teased. "Imagine if you had? You'd spend your life taking care of Flattened Boy." He lowered his voice and paraded around the car stiffly, waving his arms in wide, sweeping gestures. "Ah, well met! I'm Carson Elliott, and this is my brother, Flattened Boy...."

Carson's lips twitched. "By now Miss Buckman must be convinced you're Lunatic Boy —"

"Miss Buckman?" The smiling face was back at the window. "You're the one we've been expecting, then?"

"Ye-es, I suppose I am." Hayley feigned apprehension. She glanced at the road behind her. "Unless there's still time for retreat?"

"Not a chance." Gabriel rubbed his hands together in delight. "You're at our mercy now, Miss...Buckley?"

That's Hay-*ley* Buck-*man*," Hayley corrected him. "But you can call me Hayley, Flattened Boy." She gave Carson a look of exaggerated sympathy. "You too, Dr. Freud. However do you stand it?"

"This is nothing. You should see him when he's acting psychotic," Carson said cheerfully. "Now," he called out the window, "you might want to step aside, loon. Or I really *will* flatten you like a pancake."

Gabriel laughed. "Hardly! More likely it's her motorcar that would be done in. But all right, then. Park the old banger, and we'll give Miss —" He stopped as she gave him a speaking glance. "*Hayley* a proper look at the gardens."

"Oh, I don't know —" The weary traveler looked down upon her rumpled state. She had worn her most comfortable clothes and planned on stopping somewhere in town to put on a more presentable outfit before arriving at the manor. In the confusion, that strategy was completely forgotten. "I'm sure I should change before I —"

"Rubbish! Don't tell me you're one of those girls who's constantly bothering about how she looks? Blecch." Gabriel rolled his eyes for effect.

"Well, no. I —" she began defensively.

"All right, then. Meet you at the roundabout." Before she had a chance to argue, the boy was gone.

Hayley stared at the place where he had stood only moments before. "Well. I can see you have your hands full. That Gabriel of yours is something else."

Carson threw the car back into gear and tried to look grim. "The bane of my existence...my cross to bear...."

Hayley narrowed her eyes and peered at him more closely. "And the reason you get up every morning, unless I'm mistaken.

He's quite a boy." She smiled at what appeared to be an ill-masked expression of fondness. "I see through you, Mr. Elliott. You act all fuss and feathers, but it's obvious you love your brother very much."

"Yes, well…" Carson pulled to a stop at the crest of the circular drive. "Ah, here we are. And —" He jerked his head at the road behind them, while avoiding her gaze. "There comes your tormentor."

Hayley's door flew open as Gabriel bowed and greeted her with mock ceremony. "Welcome to Newhaven, madame."

"That's *mademoiselle*, I believe?" Carson appeared at his brother's side and turned to Hayley for confirmation. She eyed him carefully. *Was that a hint of interest?* The man remained completely unreadable.

"— mwah-zell," the boy tacked on quickly as Hayley nodded her affirmation. He gave Carson a look of wounded pride. "You didn't let me finish."

"Sorry." Carson tried to keep a straight face.

As she stood by, observing the interchange between the siblings, Hayley was struck by the obvious family resemblance. Although younger than his brother — fourteen or fifteen, Hayley guessed — and not quite as tall, Gabriel shared Carson's bright green eyes, long limbs, and shaggy, dark hair. He also had the same grasshopper look about him, further emphasized by the gawky, awkward, about-to-sprout appearance shared by young boys of all places and times.

Like most of the kids Hayley knew, Gabe favored the standard teen uniform of T-shirt and shorts; but unlike some, his clothes were in good repair — no hanging strings or gaping holes — and his shirt was devoid of made-to-shock slogans and annoying catch-phrases. Most surprising of all was his positive, friendly demeanor, so unlike that of the stereotypical, sullen American teen.

Gabriel turned back to her. "Come on. We'll help you with your things later." He grabbed one of Hayley's hands and pulled her away from the vehicle. "A-*hem*." Stepping back, he made a show of straightening an invisible tie and assumed the stance of a seasoned showman. "Ladies and Gentle —" He broke off as his gaze fell upon Carson. "And uh, you, there...the other guy." Gabriel sniffed dramatically. "Welcome to your tour of Newhaven Gardens." He paraded ahead, stepping in the direction of the colorful floral parterres. "Unless you'd rather wait for a *real* paying tour?" he threw over his shoulder, but kept walking.

"I think not." Hayley laughed and trailed after him. "You seem to me the perfect guide."

Gabriel grinned back at his brother. "I like this girl, Cars! Wherever did you find her?"

Carson walked beside Hayley, at arm's length, and gave her an assessing glance. "Er...actually, we sort of ran into each other. Or very nearly. I was just out of town when she came 'round the corner, going like old boots —"

"I *beg* your pardon." Hayley looked indignant.

"But she's a very good driver." Carson raised his eyebrows at Gabriel knowingly. "No citations."

Gabriel stopped and stared, first at Carson, then Hayley. "I've no idea what you're talking about. Are you two all right?" The younger boy shook his head sympathetically at his elders, continuing on without waiting for a response. "Senility. It's so sad."

Hayley was really amused now and followed with increasing interest. What on earth would the boy say — or do — next?

Soon they stood at the edge of the first hedge-lined path. "Oh, look!" Hayley rushed forward and knelt beside the brilliant mass of color. Gently, she drew one hand through the delicate blue and purple blossoms, closing her eyes and drawing in deep breaths of their faint perfume.

Forget-me-not. Her heart surged with a longing for family and home. If only her parents had lived long enough to see Hayley make her dream come true. *England.* After all she'd gone through, she'd finally made it on her own. And to the very area where her parents had grown up, if she was not mistaken. Although her parents rarely talked about England, Hayley vaguely recalled them mentioning the Chiltern hills — that's what had caught her fancy and inspired her to apply for the internship in the first place. What would Jon and Camilla Buckman have said if they'd known? *They never did want me to pursue gardening. But, still...I'm happy. And I'm making it...so far. Wouldn't they be proud?*

"Hayley?" She jumped as Carson's breath tickled her ear. "Sorry. Didn't mean to frighten you. For a moment there, we thought we'd lost you."

Hayley grinned sheepishly at the man and boy crouched beside her. "*Myosotis.*" She indicated the flowers with one hand. "I'm afraid I'm a sucker for them."

"Get you!" Gabriel made a face. "*My-o-so-tis.* 'Fraid the only Latin my brother and I know is *Pig-o-so-tis.* Isn't-ay *at*-thay *ight*-ray, *arson*-cay?"

Carson rolled his eyes and gave the boy a gentle shove, knocking him off balance. "*Oool*-fay."

Gabriel picked himself up off the dirt-covered path and brushed off his cotton shorts with as much dignity as he could muster. "*Ardon*-pay *ee*-may." Sticking his nose in the air, he wandered away, looking gravely offended.

Carson turned his full attention back to the woman at his side. "Are you all right?" His expression was one of genuine concern. "You're looking a little pale."

"Oh, I'm fine," she said briskly, following Gabriel's example and rising. "Just getting a little moony about home, that's all." Hayley kept her tone light and concentrated on avoiding those penetrating green eyes. "I'll be all right once I get settled." She looked ahead, keeping her young tour guide within sight. "*Abriel*-gay. Wait up!" she called, then turned to the man behind her, one eyebrow raised. "Pig Latin? Let me guess. The benefits of an American mother?"

He grinned in response. "That's right."

Hayley whistled long and low, as if terribly impressed. "My. Bilingual. How *European.*" She sighed, and ran after the young boy.

Taking the hint, Carson followed a bit more slowly. By the time he'd caught up, Gabriel already had the tour back in full swing. Hayley listened in amusement, remembering how the boy's older brother had earlier launched into a detailed explanation of the feudal system. *Must be in the blood.*

"Every one of these beds is filled with forget-me-nots," Gabriel was saying. "See there? All the way back to the road. Then there are five different colored flowers mixed in along alternating beds."

"Tulips, primroses —"

"Right. And back there," he pointed, "pansies, wallflowers,

and…sweet rocket." The young boy nodded proudly, obviously enjoying his role. Hayley couldn't help but smile.

"And what," a strange voice cut in, "is the name of this beautiful flower — this delightful new discovery who has graced us with her beauty?"

So long had it been since Hayley had found time to interact with the opposite sex, she nearly failed to realize that the reference was to her. At first, she glanced around the parterre, ignorantly trying to image which lovely blossom might be new, then — as realization dawned — turned wide eyes upon the newcomer.

Hayley could not imagine why she hadn't noticed the stranger approach; he was not an individual who could easily be missed. Taller even than her new gardening partner, he appeared to stand about six-foot-four. But impressive height was the least of his attention-grabbing features. Hayley could not remember when she had seen a more attractive man. A strong, chiseled jaw set off his almost too-handsome face, and dark, professionally-coifed hair fell artistically across his brow. Clearly poised and sophisticated — even in silence — he somehow managed to make his presence tangibly felt without speaking. The man posed a striking figure, appearing even more masculine in contrast to the floral background against which he stood.

Hayley waited for one of her companions to offer an introduction; to her surprise, both remained uncharacteristically speechless. *Thanks a lot, guys.* She gathered her composure.

"I'm — no flower, I'm afraid. Hayley Buckman," she smiled, "from the States."

"And people say nothing good comes from America." The

man exuded warmth and charm. "It's a pleasure to meet you, Miss Buckman." He inclined his head graciously.

"And you are...?" But before she could continue, Carson uttered something unintelligible.

"What's that?" The stranger turned to Carson, his voice sharp.

The lanky gardener blinked, looking unruffled. "Why, nothing."

From his position nearby, Gabriel shrugged. "I didn't hear anything," he agreed. Man and boy exchanged looks of innocence.

The dark-haired stranger was clearly irritated. "I am," he turned back to Hayley, "Evan Harrington. Nephew, of a distant sort, to Theadora Harrington. And you are the new gardening expert we've been waiting for? How wonderful. Lord knows we need someone with skill," he said pointedly.

Carson bristled visibly but held his tongue.

"Uh, I wouldn't call myself an expert." Hayley looked uncertainly from one man to the other. "But I can assure you, the pleasure is all mine."

"Not *all*," the handsome newcomer proclaimed gallantly, stepping forward to take her hand. When he spoke again, his voice was low, and steely gray eyes gazed deeply into hers. "I can assure you...the pleasure is most definitely not *all* yours."

She swallowed hard and stared at the man, unsure of how to react. The compliment was a bit much, especially considering their lack of relationship. But there was something about the man's playful charm that drew her. Whether it was his laughing eyes or simply the fact that Hayley was enjoying the adventure of visiting a foreign country, she could not help but feel amused. She could think of no one else who could get away with such outrageous flattery.

Was he serious? Surely he was harmless. Yet as a Harrington, she knew, he might have certain influence over her career. And if the effect on her rapidly-beating heart was any indication, she realized in alarm, her career wasn't the only thing he might influence. She felt slightly weak-kneed at being the focus of attention for such a handsome man. Hayley was apparently more vulnerable to men than she'd thought; she would have to tread carefully.

Carson could stand it no longer. "Good grief, Harrington!" he exploded. "You really *are* a piece of work, aren't you?" The men eyed each other warily, like two lions preparing to battle for leadership of the pride. After a moment, Carson switched his gaze and stared pointedly at Hayley's graceful hand, still held tightly in Evan's grasp. Hayley registered his desperate glance, but could not discern how he expected her to react. After a slight hesitation, the gardener turned his icy glare upon her face.

"When you're done being *pawed* by the boss's leeching nephew-twenty-times-removed, Miss Buckman, you can let me know. Maybe then we can get some work done." Spinning on his heel, he stormed back in the direction of the car.

Hayley stared, openmouthed, at his retreating form. "Wha —?" She turned back to the two remaining. Evan wore an ill-concealed look of disgust, while Gabriel seemed to have found something of profound interest stuck to the bottom of one shoe.

"I'm sure I can't imagine." Harrington smoothly drew her hand through the crook of his arm and began to lead her deeper into the gardens. "Shall we continue with your tour?"

From behind them, Gabriel piped up, "Great! I was just getting started." He smiled brightly and matched Hayley's step.

She glanced at the expression of irritation evident on the sophisticated man's face. Obviously, Evan Harrington was not practiced at hiding his feelings, but at least he refrained from verbally expressing them.

"Oh, boy," she managed, without much enthusiasm. "This is going to be great. Just...great."

Five

❧

Round and round the circle / Completing the charm...
T.S. Eliot, *La Figlia Che Piange*

Despite the obvious tension between her two distinctly different escorts, Hayley brightened at the prospect of the sea of beauty which she knew most certainly lay ahead. She turned to the handsome man at her side, determined not to let Carson's outburst cast a shadow over the realization of her long-held dream.

"Tell me, Mr. Harrington," she said with a smile intended to set him at ease, "what it's like to live in paradise?"

Her companion reciprocated the warm look. "Actually, I keep a flat in London. And I'd hardly call that paradise." Harrington grimaced good-naturedly. "But I drive up often enough to have developed an appreciation for true beauty." He looked at her pointedly, with eyes that expressed profound admiration. "Trust me. I *do* know beauty when I see it."

Hayley almost laughed out loud before she realized that the man was serious. She bit her lip and gave the newcomer more careful consideration.

Never before had she met a man who seemed more sure of

himself. But then, her experience with men didn't go much further than a few high school friendships and a smattering of ill-fated, short-term relationships in college.

Hayley wasn't sure why her love life had been so uneventful. It wasn't for lack of example; her parents had a strong, loving relationship. Nor could it be blamed on a failure to attract. Both Jon and Camilla Buckman had been stunning in their youth and had remained handsome adults. Although Hayley did not often think about her appearance and did not consider herself overwhelmingly beautiful, she knew that her resemblance to both parents assured that she was certainly not *un*attractive. The looks of interest she regularly received from the opposite sex confirmed this fact.

On the other hand, Hayley was never big on flirting. Although she was a bubbly and outgoing teenager who hadn't lacked for friends, she'd never felt especially interested in any young man and had rarely given a boy reason to believe she might welcome his attentions. There *was* the especially persistent young fullback Hayley had dated during her freshman year of college. But after a couple of months and a few shared kisses, Hayley knew she didn't love him and had gently broken off the relationship. Subsequent attempts at dating were even less successful. And several years later, after listening to the anguished stories of lovelorn college girlfriends, she'd become less inclined than ever to open herself up to heartache.

She thought back on the dozens of beautiful, intelligent, loving young girls she knew who had thrown themselves into relationships with boys who were emotionally withdrawn or noncommittal: young men who seemed unwilling to extend themselves to the point of truly knowing another person or sharing feelings of real depth. Surely, she had often wondered, there was more to a relationship than that? Looking at the man who now walked beside her, she saw no such lack of confidence. *Is non-commitment just an American phenomenon?* This stranger certainly seemed willing to lay his feelings — or at least his opinions — on the line. Despite herself, Hayley felt slightly impressed.

In her heart, Hayley knew that her avoidance of relationships had less to do with her friends' heartbreaks than it did with her own fear of abandonment. After her parents' deaths, she had purposefully thrown herself into her studies. Self-imposed isolation had become a place of safety. But somehow in this new place, Hayley didn't feel so safe anymore.

Resting her eyes upon a giant, but artfully-trimmed yew, Hayley suddenly realized that the box herb hedges and delicate multi-colored blossoms now lay behind them. Beneath her feet, the white stone path continued past the great floral parterre toward a five-foot wall built from bricks of various shades of red: many a deep, rich orange, others nearly black — most splattered with patches of white mortar. From the angle at which she stood, Hayley could not see through the wall's opening; she closed her eyes and tried to imagine the ocean of color and fragrance which would soon overwhelm her senses.

"Hayley?" Gabriel reached out and tugged on her hand.

She blinked at the teenager in surprise, having almost forgotten about his presence.

"You look funny again," he accused. "Are you sure you're okay?"

Hayley had to smile; it had been a long time since she was the object of anyone's worry. That it came from such a young boy made the sentiment even more sweet.

She squeezed his hand in appreciation. "I've never been better, Gabriel!" The contentment in her eyes was real. "It's just that…oh, so many moments go too quickly. I want this one to last." The look she gave him was an appeal for understanding. "You know?"

Gabriel lowered his eyes, apparently reluctant to admit to such sentiment in front of the other man. But he did manage to nod and mumble quietly, "Yeah, I know. Things do disappear awful fast." He pulled his hand away and with a look of disdain for Evan Harrington, turned and pounded back down the path.

Hayley watched him go. "He's…a sad boy, isn't he?" The question didn't require a response.

Her companion answered anyway. "Both of the Elliotts are a little…*off*, if you ask me." His voice held a trace of contempt.

"*Off?* In what way, off?" Hayley looked at him curiously.

"Just…" The man paused. "Oh, I don't know," he continued, shrugging. "I guess *bitter* would be a better word. They're pleasant enough when things are going their way. But when the going gets difficult, they can't really seem to accept it. Everyone else is at fault in their eyes, and I think that they'd like to see the whole world pay. Especially the older one. I'd be careful if I were you," he warned. "You'll be working with the man —" He stopped, taking her expression to be one of alarm. "Oh, now I'm sure that you'll be safe enough —" Hayley resisted the urge to roll her eyes. *What is that? The Newhaven motto?* "— but I wouldn't…you know. Get too close." He lowered his voice on the last word for emphasis.

Hayley's eyes narrowed. "Excuse me? I'm sure I don't know what you mean."

"Please don't misinterpret." He flashed her a devastating smile that made her spine tingle and even made her forget her momentary flicker of irritation. "I'm not trying to make any implications or wild assumptions. It's simply —" He stopped and seemed to weigh his words.

Small, tanned hands rested on her slim hips. "Yes? Go on."

Her companion sighed. "You're angry now, and that's the last thing I intended. All right. I'll tell you…although this is hardly the conversation to be having upon your arrival. I'd hate to have you running back to London before first light."

Hayley resisted the urge to smile. "I can assure you, that's hardly likely," she said ruefully, reflecting on her earlier experience with the Mini.

The man missed her meaning completely. "Well…as you say. I'm sure you're not one to be easily frightened. It's just that the woman who was here before you —"

"Francine," Hayley supplied.

"Er, yes." Something flashed in his steely gray eyes. Clearly, the man was used to being in complete control of every situation; his look of surprise could almost be taken for one of panic. "Francine. However did you hear about her?"

"Carson told me her name," Hayley admitted. "And in her letter, Theodora Harrington mentioned that the woman who had been here was called away rather unexpectedly."

"Of course." Harrington still looked perplexed. "But you've…not met her then?" He peered around as if he half-expected an apparition to float up from behind one of the larger bushes.

"Oh, no." Hayley shook her head, trying not to laugh at his

confusion. "Nothing like that." The man relaxed visibly. "Why on earth do you ask?"

Finally, the humor of the situation seemed to dawn on him, and his strong, well-defined mouth broke into a generous smile. "I must certainly appear the fool! I must admit, the whole thing has set my teeth on edge." He sobered and as he leaned closer to her ear, Hayley felt the touch of his breath on her cheek and shuddered involuntarily. "It was quite odd how Francine came to leave us," he spoke in a low voice. "Very mysterious."

Gray eyes gazed deeply into hers. "You see, Francine was supposed to stay through June. Her departure was very abrupt. There wasn't a hint that she was unhappy; she never said a word to anyone about leaving. We had no clue why she would go like that. That's why I can't help but think —" He glanced behind them, seeming to try to ascertain how far Gabriel had gone back down the path. Apparently deciding it was safe to speak, he continued in hushed tones, "Well, she was very close with your gardener friend. And I'll admit, he's not a man I particularly trust. I can't help but wonder if there's some connection."

Hayley took a small step backward, trying to digest the information. "*My* gardener friend?"

"Sorry. I didn't mean anything by that. I.... Just promise me that you'll be careful?" He flashed her a winning smile.

Hayley stood stunned, not knowing how to answer. The man appeared genuinely concerned. Carson hadn't struck her as being any kind of threat. But, then, she didn't really know him. She didn't know any of them....

"And I was the one who convinced Aunt Theadora that

Francine wouldn't be back," Harrington was saying. He threw back his head and laughed. "Imagine if Francine *had* returned, and just as you were arriving? Now wouldn't *that* be awkward!" He seemed quite amused at the prospect. "Aunt Theadora doesn't like it when —" He looked thoughtful. "Well, let's just say that it is much more pleasant at Newhaven when things are going smoothly."

One graceful eyebrow raised: half in concern, half in amusement. "Should I be worried?"

"You?" Evan Harrington reached out and drew her small hands into his. "*You*, Miss Buckman, are a delight. I am certain that you will do quite famously."

"Well, I don't know if I'm a delight," Hayley said, laughing. "But I *am* a hard worker. And I promise that what I lack in knowledge I more than make up for with enthusiasm. Plus," she pulled her hands from his grasp and wiggled her fingers in the air, "I know I've got at least *one* green thumb. I haven't killed a plant yet!"

"And a beautiful thumb it is." The man knew how to deliver a compliment, but he also knew when to back off. The look he gave her was sincerely appreciative but carefully non-threatening, and he did not attempt to initiate further physical contact. "Come on. The Formal Garden is just ahead," he informed her, proceeding down the white stone path. "I think this moment has lasted long enough, don't you?"

Hayley followed with a grin. "So you were listening to Gabriel and me? Is that what this was all about? All right, all right. You've done your duty. I'm ready." She approached with a renewed sense of anticipation. "I hope it's everything it's cracked up to b —" As she drew closer, a slow smile of delight spread across her face, causing her gently curved cheeks to dimple.

At the garden's entrance, a beautiful white wooden gate, topped by elegant *fleurs-de-lis* scrollwork, stood open wide, beckoning for her to step within the walls of warm-toned brick. Hayley did so without further hesitation.

Inside, a vast expanse of verdant lawn spread out before Hayley, inviting her, she imagined, to kick off her shoes and run free as a child. For just a moment, she closed her eyes, and her delicate lips curved upward as she thought of doing exactly that. But moments later, as she glanced around once more, it was the glorious herbaceous border which caught and held her eye.

The traditional deep herbaceous border, Hayley knew, had been an element of English gardens since Tudor times but had become increasingly popular at the turn of the century and was, in fact, considered by many to capture the very essence of the English garden. The borders at Newhaven were clearly no exception.

All around the garden's edge, the melody of beauty and harmony of peace seemed to rise and blend in a symphony of shape and color. Spectacular delphiniums, gentle garden pinks, graceful columbine.... Each cluster spilled into the next; Hayley's eye could barely discern where one group of flowers ended and the next tangle began.

Mentally, she ticked off the different types of plants, many not yet blooming: annuals, biennials, perennials, bulbs...a smattering of mixed shrubs and bush roses.... Clearly, the border was not designed to fit the strictest definition of "herbaceous": any plant that was leafy, herb-like, or as characterized by some, "not woody." Newhaven's gardeners were generous — and wise, Hayley thought — in their choice of flower and foliage. Judging from the variety of plants represented just in the first few feet, it was clear that these gardens were in no danger of having a limited peak season. Expansion of plant selection had been a growing trend; Hayley was pleased to see the practice had caught on at Newhaven.

She turned her attention to the garden's inner circle: a striking contrast to the wild borders that first captured her attention. While the outer beds were designed to represent an unrestrained mix of genus and species, the inner strips reflected both control and order. Row after row of neatly planted bulbs, already blooming, curved around the square garden, divided into quarter-sections by lush, grassy walkways, like four enormous pieces of pie. The flowers were large, their heads seemingly too long for their stalks; several bowed and smiled a benevolent welcome on the newcomers.

Toward the center of the garden, about halfway down each piece of "pie," curved a row of cypress hedges that had been clipped into a variety of geometrical and representational forms: a ship, a turtle, a star.... Hayley smiled. *Tourists — especially the children — must love those.* Within that circle stood a row of majestic, thriving yews she guessed to be nearly three hundred years old.

Hayley stepped down the path. "What's at the center, inside the circle of yews?"

Evan shrugged. "Not much. A few smaller rows of dwarf daffodils and polyanthus. Mostly it's a nice place to walk in the shade. There used to be a statue at the center, but it's long gone." He eyed her closely. "Did you want to look?"

Stopping long enough to consider his offer, Hayley suddenly realized how tired she was — and how inappropriately she was dressed.

"Actually…I think I'd rather pick up my things at the car and find my room before anyone else sees me." She looked down in remorse at her sloppy attire. How was it possible that this man had been so complimentary? "Are you sure you aren't humiliated at the prospect of being seen in the presence of this hideous Yank?"

Her smooth-talking companion turned on the charm once more. "Nonsense. You, my hideous Yank, are the most beautiful flower in this garden." His smile seemed to shine several shades brighter than the weak English sun. "May I?" He offered Hayley his arm, and to her surprise, she found herself accepting. "Come on." He stepped back in the direction from which they had come. "Your 'new haven' awaits." And he grinned at his own wit.

Six

❦

Very nice sort of place...I should think,
for people that like that sort of place.
George Bernard Shaw, *Man and Superman*

B right, red faces tilted upward from the crystal pitcher, as if begging for a smile...or a kiss.

Hayley paused, one hand poised over her open suitcase, and leaned closer to the honeysuckle beckoning from the vanity beside her, breathing deeply of its heady fragrance. Closing her eyelids part-way, she gave in to the childish impulse to brush the trumpet-shaped blossoms with her own full lips, then jumped back, startled, after pricking her skin on a spike of fresh, green rosemary. She smiled and moved back to her travel bag, lying open on the bed.

It was a good sign, Hayley reflected while unfolding a crushed linen vest, to find the beautiful arrangement awaiting her. Certainly Theodora Harrington had not picked the flowers herself; but perhaps she *had* given orders for the bouquet to be placed in the new intern's living quarters. In keeping with her general practice of assuming the best, Hayley determined to consider it a special gesture.

And even if it's not, she told herself, *I'm lucky to be staying in the main house at all.* Nothing in Theadora's earlier communications had indicated what sort of housing Hayley could expect. Somehow, she had imagined herself in a small, dilapidated cottage without heat or running water. *Perhaps I have read a few too many gothic novels!* For a moment, her imagination ran wild as she pictured herself in heavy black period dress: an eighteenth century governess arriving at Newhaven, hoping to be well-received by the affluent and elegant Harringtons...praying for the family's generous acceptance...unintentionally — and disastrously — falling in love with the young lord of the estate.... *In this case, it would have to be the nephew to the lady of the manor.*

She laughed out loud, suddenly struck by the humor of the thought. She and Evan Harrington? Ridiculous. She barely knew the man. But he was obviously an overly-confident, though harmless, flirt. Although she found it impossible to take him seriously, Hayley could not help but wonder what was behind his attentions. *What could he possibly want with me...the new gardener? He's handsome, wealthy...from a prominent family....* Despite the fact that he was obviously not the man for her, Hayley had to admit that it had felt wonderful to bask in the glow of his attention, even if only briefly.

She glanced up from her work and took another assessing look around the room that was to be — as Evan had punned — her personal "new haven."

Had she been given an opportunity to speculate on the guest room's probable decor, Hayley would likely have predicted a Laura Ashley-type blend of romantic fabrics, furniture, and wall coverings: a style she could appreciate, but which was very different from that which she had chosen for her own small, artistically-decorated home. Indeed, her assigned room did reflect an extravagant mood, but to her surprise, the design was more in line with her personal taste for bold colors and patterns than she might reasonably have expected.

Overall, the chamber reflected a bright garden theme, the irony of which did not escape Hayley's notice. The Chinese-patterned wallpaper which set the room's tone featured a background of rich, bay leaf green. But it was the wild Chinoiserie design which commanded the visitor's attention: beady-eyed partridges perched on thick, leafy branches; daring, yellow chrysanthemums; brilliant gold and vivid blue Monarchs, captured mid-flight.

Hanging on either side of the tall windows were elegant drapes in soft, muted shades of brown. Even the furnishings were of neutral, subdued earth tones, so as not to compete with the brighter wall scheme. Whoever decorated the room, Hayley imagined, clearly intended for the chamber to reflect the balance of peace and freedom that was part of the very best gardens.

With one quick, final-sounding zip, Hayley shut her leather bag and stepped over to the vanity to tackle the task of pulling herself together before tea.

"Take all the time you need," Evan had offered generously, after showing her to her room. "But please do join me downstairs at four." His eyes twinkled. "It's been ages since we've had such a charming guest, and I refuse to waste a single moment of your stay."

Hayley smoothed her thick, snarled hair with one hand while giving her travel-weary reflection a look of disgust.

"Mr. Harrington," she chided the absent man, "you *really* must get out more."

Having done her best to restore some semblance of order to her appearance, Hayley took a deep breath and mentally prepared to face whatever dragons lay in wait. With one last look of longing, she left her cheerful room, stepped into the timber-paneled hallway, and carefully retraced the path by which Evan had led her one hour earlier. Soon, she found herself at the head of the sweeping oak staircase; as she descended, her eyes scanned the expansive hall below.

Perhaps the chamber's most striking element was its size. Reaching two stories high and stretching over one hundred feet in length, its very essence was that of opulence and dignity. The staircase, too, was grand in both design and scale. Beneath Hayley's hand, a smoothly polished balustrade stretched the full length of the upper balcony, turned, extended eight or nine steps to the lower landing, rotated again, then repeated the pattern one last time before reaching the ground floor.

Despite its high, open ceilings and expansive dimensions, the oak-paneled great hall maintained a presence that was both dark and foreboding. A scarcity of furniture further detracted from the warmth of the room, its only adornment being several elegant French-style chairs, a number of dark-toned Oriental carpets, and several gilt-framed portraits of somber-looking lords and ladies Hayley could not — and had no desire to — identify.

Stepping across the hard, stone floor, Hayley felt herself drawn instinctively to the doorway to the right, from which gleamed the faintest hint of sunlight. As she entered, she found herself, once again, in the midst of a decadently opulent room, complete with ornate carved wall panels, gold-trimmed built-in bookshelves, an elaborate stone fireplace, and splendidly gaudy tapestries. But although the parlor's basic design was as impressive as that of the main hall, its furnishings had been planned with a more humble visitor in mind, and Hayley spied several pieces, including an overstuffed ochre sofa, upon which she could imagine herself feeling reasonably comfortable.

"Ah, there you are!" a friendly voice called. "I'd just come looking for you."

Turning to greet her host, Hayley nearly stared. It hadn't been her imagination: the man was even more handsome than she remembered.

Evan Harrington had looked incredibly attractive in his business clothing; dressed casually for tea, he was devastating. Gone were the conventional navy suit and dark overcoat; in their place, he wore stone-colored chinos and an Italian wool shirt of black and charcoal houndstooth that exactly matched the gray of his eyes.

He stepped forward, grinning confidently, as if he were reading Hayley's thoughts.

"You look beautiful," he said in a voice like silk. "Much more…refreshed."

It was true. In her white tailored blouse and swingy tarragon-print skirt, Hayley appeared fashionable, professional, and completely put-together.

"Well, at least I'm presentable," she conceded.

"You needn't have gone to the trouble on my account," Evan offered, "although I do appreciate the effect. But it looks as though I may be the only one you'll be 'presenting' yourself to this afternoon."

"Really?" Hayley tried to sound disappointed, but relief

must have been clearly written on her face. "Is Mrs.—Lady Harrington — ill?"

"Oh, no." He shrugged, obviously unconcerned. "Just… moody."

"Moody. How?" Hopeful images of a benevolent Theadora Harrington drifted away like mist.

"Don't fret about Aunt Theadora," Evan assured her comfortingly. "She isn't happy unless she has you on edge. Makes her feel in control." He pulled Hayley's hand into the crook of his arm and led her toward a beamed archway at the far end of the parlor. "Theadora's a contrary thing. If it had *not* been proper for her to greet you, I can assure you that's exactly where she would have been."

"She sounds terribly…difficult," Hayley managed nervously.

Evan nodded approvingly. "There. You see? You understand her perfectly." The words were light-hearted, but his tone was cynical.

He directed Hayley through the elegant doorway and onto a shady, tree-lined terrace, scented by a unique perfume from the surrounding dogwoods, lilacs, and other flowering shrubs. Looking out onto the grounds, Hayley saw that a level lawn had been cut into the hillside below. A flight of stone steps led in the direction of the formal gardens; she could just make out the brick walkway and the tops of the yews. Along the subsequent path extended two long rows of rose bushes that had not yet bloomed, but would soon be a wonderful tangle of fragrance and color.

Evan led Hayley to a charming, white wrought-iron table and pulled out her chair before seating himself. Moments later, as if she had been waiting in the wings, a timid maid appeared and placed before them an exquisite silver tea set, the tea board heaped with fresh hot scones, butter, strawberry jam, and Devonshire cream.

Following her host's lead, Hayley took one biscuit from the heavily-laden tray and spread it with a thick layer of butter and jam.

"So tell me, Evan," she urged, "how *are* you related to Theadora Harrington? You said you're a nephew of a sort. What sort is that, exactly?" She popped one steaming morsel into her mouth and sighed in pleasure as the pastry melted against her tongue.

"All right, you asked for it," Evan warned. "Advanced Harrington Genealogy is now in session." He grinned. "Actually, it's not all that complicated. You see, my great-grandfather was Edward Harrington. You may have seen his portrait in the main hall?"

Hayley shook her head but did not answer, her mouth full of crumbs.

"Well," Evan continued, "Theadora married his son David. David's younger brother was my grandfather, Michael. Naturally, Newhaven passes on through the eldest son. Newhaven should have gone to Theadora and David's heirs. Unfortunately, they didn't have any. My own father died a few years ago. Sometimes I think how odd it is that I should be an heir. I'm not even Theadora's nephew, really. More like a second nephew. But there you have it."

"How sad." Hayley thought back to her own childhood: being first-generation immigrants from England, her parents had no relatives in America. As a result, Hayley had no aunts, uncles, cousins, or other extended family. She'd missed those relationships but had always been close to her parents. Living without heirs — any direct blood relation at all — somehow seemed much worse.

Evan's steely gray eyes held no trace of compassion. "Oh, I wouldn't worry about Theadora. She does fine on her own."

"'On her own.' She hasn't a husband any more, then?"

The man shook his head. "Widowed. Three years now. Uncle David was probably the only person in this world who had a personality stronger than Theadora's."

Hayley eyed him closely. His manicured hands rested against the table; there was no sign that his words were sparked by a feeling of irritation or frustration over a particular event. The man appeared to be matter-of-factly relating what he saw to be true. "You don't like her very much, do you?"

Evan stared out across the smooth, terraced lawn, apparently unconcerned by the question. "It's not a matter of 'like' or 'dislike' with Theadora," he said, his voice cool. "It's a matter of watching out for one's own needs."

Hayley did not understand his inference, but did not question it, instinctively knowing she would not like the answer she might receive. Trying to change the subject, she wondered aloud, "So you're all she has, then?"

"Oh, no!" Evan laughed and turned back to the tea tray, spooning into the jam. "You haven't met the brains of the family, my brother, Simon. He drove into London to pick up his fiancée, Isabelle, for the weekend. I expect they should be back sometime later tonight."

"The brains, huh?" Hayley took the bait. "What are you, then?"

The man leaned forward and whispered conspiratorially, "Ah. I'm the beauty."

She rolled her eyes in mock disgust. "Good thing you're not the humility. *Or* the tact."

Evan glanced back toward the manor house, his eyes widening slightly. *"Or* the judgment. It looks like I was way off concerning my brother. *Simon!"* This he directed over her shoulder.

Hayley turned in her seat and was struck by the sight of what appeared to be a younger, slimmer version of the man at her table. Sharp, well-defined features marked a face that, while not as rugged-looking as that of Evan Harrington's, was strong in its own simple way. The gray eyes, too, were familiar, although Evan's were of a steely intensity — and at times, could almost be perceived as cold — while Simon's had a gentle look about them.

Facial structure was not all that the two brothers had in common; fashion sense was clearly a consistent family trait. Despite the fact he had just driven up from London, Simon looked cool and comfortable in his stonewashed, forest oxford and canvas trousers. Although his image was less like that of a model and more like one of the "frat boys" from Hayley's college campus, the confidence and physical family resemblance he shared with Evan were undeniable.

Beside him was a tall, thin woman, all golden hair and lean limbs. She was inarguably beautiful, with thin, high-arched eyebrows that gave her the appearance of one perpetually asking Why? and her skin already glowed with a lovely, warm tan, even in early spring.

The woman appeared to be a perfect match to the dapper Harrington to whom she now clung. Sleek and sophisticated in a white, scoop-necked tank, dark, wool crepe skirt and matching jacket, and stacked heel mules, she obviously shared his classic tastes. And from the look of adoration she was giving her fiancé, it was clear she was thrilled just to be in his presence. Only her youth gave Hayley momentary pause in reflecting upon the probable success of their union.

"Greetings, brother!" Evan stood, stepped across the terrace, and clapped his brother a bit roughly on the back. "I thought you were spending the afternoon in the city."

"That was our intention." Simon's voice was gentle and rich in timbre. "But Isabelle wanted to get out of London. Isn't that right, Issy?" He turned to the woman at his side.

The striking blonde looked somewhat skeptical, but seemed unwilling to argue the point. "It's quite crowded," she offered non-committally, tucking a second hand under the fold of his sleeve.

"Well, it's smashing that you're here now. You're just in time to meet our guest, Miss Hayley Buckman." Evan turned and gave her a small half-bow.

Hayley stood with a laugh and greeted the newcomer graciously. "It's such a pleasure to meet you, Mr. Harrington."

Extricating himself from the tall woman's grip, Simon stepped forward and offered Hayley his hand, which she shook, then quickly released. "It is a pleasure indeed." The words and delivery were smooth; the man was a Harrington to the bone. Nervously the blonde moved up to join him and took his hand once more. "And…this is my fiancée, Isabelle Chevalier."

The woman nodded coolly.

"How do you do?" Hayley smiled politely, then turned back

to the woman's escort, artfully ignoring the rebuff. "Will you join us for tea?"

Simon seemed poised to accept, then paused and glanced down at the hand on his arm. "Actually, no. We've just gotten in, ourselves, and I'd like to get Isabelle settled. Some other time, perhaps?"

"Of course."

From Simon, Hayley received one last smile; from Isabelle, one final glare.

"Brother." Evan nodded casually at the younger man.

"Brother." Simon grinned and followed his fiancée into the house.

Hayley stared after them. "Was it something I said?"

"Said?" Evan laughed. "I think not. I dare say it's how you look. Isabelle was positively green."

The young woman stared at him unbelieving. "What? Surely you're joking. Jealous of me? That breathtaking creature?"

Evan sighed dramatically. "I'm afraid Isabelle's lack of confidence throws a bit of a shadow over her beauty."

"Well, she needn't worry about me," Hayley insisted. "I'm here for one reason, and one reason only. And it *isn't* to catch her man — or any other." She reseated herself at the iron table and broke a scone in two.

"Really? How *very* interesting." Evan moved to join her, a look of challenge in his eyes. "And for what reason *are* you here?"

Hayley looked incredulous. "Why, to complete my internship, of course."

"Of course," Evan agreed amicably, stirring his tea. Then, after a moment of thought, "This should prove to be quite a summer...quite a summer indeed."

Seven

'*Speak when you are spoken to!*'
the Red Queen sharply interrupted her.
Lewis Carroll, *Through the Looking Glass*

Hayley stirred beneath the great, white lace comforter under which she had burrowed and yawned widely. Extending one sleep-heavy arm, then the other, she made a valiant effort to stretch herself into wakefulness. This was one morning she could not afford to lounge about in bed. She glanced at the clock. No danger there. It was barely 6:00 A.M. She always made an effort to turn in early, but last night had been ridiculous. After spending nearly an hour in Evan's undiluted company, listening to him ramble on about the manor's long history, Hayley had actually started to nod in her chair. Excusing herself, she'd gone to her room, hoping to catch a nap; exhausted after traveling throughtout the previous night, she'd slept clear through until morning.

As prior communication was sparse, she had no idea what was expected of her that day; when she'd asked, Evan seemed as unable to predict the next day's events as she. Whether she would be working in the gardens, meeting with the mysterious Theadora Harrington, or simply familiarizing herself with the grounds, Hayley knew she would have to gather up all her energy and fortitude. She would need both if she were to stick to the resolution she had made the night before: not to allow herself to be drawn any further into Evan Harrington's little game of flirtation.

Any other course of action would be foolish. Evan evidently had serious issues with his aunt, Hayley's employer. Even clearer was the tension between him and the man she would be working with most directly. Besides, Evan Harrington was charming, but Hayley doubted that he was a man of depth. If there was one thing she had learned from observing her parents, it was that the keys to a lasting, loving relationship were character and faith. That's what Hayley desired for her own life. Not that she, herself, had been particularly faithful since her parents' deaths, Hayley thought ruefully. At the same time, she knew better than to get involved with someone who didn't share her belief system…no matter how far buried it might lie. *Fun's fun, but this has gone far enough,* she thought. The attention was flattering, but it was time to remind Evan Harrington of the limits to their relationship.

She groaned and kicked her feet over the edge of the enormous maple four-poster, wincing as they met the morning-chilled floorboards. The clothes she'd picked out the night before lay waiting for her: worn, waffle-soled work boots, nutmeg-colored jersey, and casual tan trousers — perfect for work or play; Hayley hoped it would be the former. She needed to throw herself into her gardening. Already, her visit to Newhaven had been vastly more emotionally draining than she could have ever anticipated.

And today wouldn't likely be any easier.

Descending the gleaming staircase as she had the previous afternoon, Hayley was surprised to find, once more, what appeared to be a completely empty house. Her footsteps echoed as they struck the smooth, gray flagstones of the great hall. Looking for someone who might direct her toward her breakfast, she stepped timidly into the grand dining room: a monstrous, garish affair abundant with gilded mirrors, sweeping red drapes, and elegant chairs of a French provincial design.

The effect was impressive, but hardly welcoming, and Hayley squelched the desire to mumble something uncomplimentary. The way sound carried in old manor houses, there was no telling who might overhear.

"Miss?" The timid maid of the previous day was back, although this time, she seemed not nearly as reticent. "I'll bring your breakfast, if you'd like to wait on the terrace."

"That would be wonderful." Hayley gratefully followed the woman out of the chamber. Minutes later, she found herself listening to the song of a lark while enjoying a deep bowl of porridge, toast, and marmalade. To her relief, Evan Harrington did not make an appearance, nor did his younger counterpart or the chilly Isabelle. After filling herself with two bowls of the oatmeal and cream and licking the last of the sweet preserves from her sticky fingers, Hayley felt well-fortified and ready to face the day.

She ventured down the white stone footpath, in the direction of the formal gardens, and as she walked, found herself scanning the terraced lawns and decorative beds, hoping to catch a glimpse of at least one of the Elliott brothers. Although the path was different from the one she had taken with the two upon her arrival and the surrounding lawns and roses a departure from the bright floral parterres, this path, like the first, proceeded directly toward the now-familiar brick wall: obviously the center of focus for the entire estate. *All roads lead to Rome....*

To the south, the Chiltern hills rose like large bumps in the flat English topography. Coming from the West, Hayley could hardly be impressed by their height. But their simple beauty was undeniable. Though the land appeared, at least at that time, unoccupied, she could easily picture in her mind's eye a flock of soulful-eyed sheep roaming freely. She chuckled. *It would be hard to imagine something like that in L.A.*

As she reached the wall, she placed one hand lightly upon the ironwork of the gate, which opened easily under her touch. She paused and listened carefully; as she had hoped, a low rumble of voices rose from the center of the garden.

"Hello?" she called out timidly. Now that her wish was about to come true, Hayley suddenly had second thoughts. What if they expected her to remain indoors until summoned? Some might not appreciate the intrusion of a nosy newcomer who hadn't the grace to wait patiently.

Then again, her parents had always taught her the importance of being proactive. "Don't let life just happen to you, Hayley," her father had warned. "You've got to go out and make things happen. In business, and in life." If there were any unpardonable sins in the Buckman household, they were laziness and apathy.

Hayley kept walking, and the voices grew louder. But soon, it became apparent that the reason was not *just* that she was drawing closer. As she stepped past a bed of bright yellow bulbs and neared the row of cypress, Hayley realized in dismay that the voices coming from beyond the yews were raised in anger.

"I just want to know what you're really up to." The man was clearly agitated. "This whole thing stinks, and it's obvious you're the one making the calls."

Hayley stopped dead in her tracks. The voice that responded was clearly a woman's, although the exact words were unintelligible.

"No, this *has* nothing to do with that other 'affair,' as you put it." The man's words were biting. "The only common factor is that *one* particular person is again making his presence felt. I hardly see how what happened before affected you. In fact, you made it perfectly clear that it did *not* by refusing to get involved." The woman began to protest, but the man spoke right over her. "No, you did *not*. But this has your fingerprints all over it. And I want to know why. Just what do you stand to gain from all this, Theadora? Whatever it is, you're *not* going to get away with it."

Theadora.... Hayley held her breath. She knew she should step away, but somehow could not bring herself to move.

Apparently, the woman did not appreciate being interrupted; her voice rose by several degrees. "You forget yourself, young man! Do you realize to whom you are speaking?" She sounded shocked at the gall of her attacker. "I *will not tolerate* this sort of behavior. Not from you, not from anyone. I resent your implications...and I *refuse* to dignify your accusations with an answer. This is *my* home...for that matter, *my* garden. My affairs are mine alone. You cannot even tend to your own personal business." Her tone was icy. "I suggest you keep yourself from interfering with mine." The thick, green lawn effectively muffled any sound of footsteps, but based on the finality and drama in her tone, Hayley guessed the woman was making a theatrical exit. The only question was: Which direction was she going?

Oh, Lord, please help me.... Hayley glanced around frantically, searching for a place to hide. Her choices were limited, if not nonexistent. The herbaceous borders were too far away and offered almost no cover. The flower beds were worthless in terms of protection. The yews were perfect, but by diving into them, she would effectively be jumping directly into Theadora's arms.

Her only other option was the topiary. Casting her eye upon one large cypress sailing ship, Hayley threw herself upon it and tried to align her body behind the large, artfully-clipped bough 'mast.'

In the distance, crashing branches and muttered words of wrath made it easy to follow the retreat of the opposing party. But from her position, Hayley could neither see nor hear whether Theadora had left the grounds. She pinched her eyes shut and forced herself to take shallow breaths, resisting the urge to peer around the cypress sail.

After what seemed like several long minutes of silence, Hayley decided that the woman had simply exited from another gate. Smiling at her foolishness, she had just made up her mind to 'disembark' when a dry-sounding voice announced, "It doesn't go anywhere, you know."

Hayley froze, one leg poised mid-air. Ever so slowly, she turned her face until she had the voice's originator within her line of sight. Her worst fears were confirmed; the figure she spotted was a woman: graying, sharp-eyed, and thin. Dressed in a dark linen pantsuit and heavy, loose-knit sweater to ward off the spring chill, she was the picture of casual nobility. Her expression was unreadable: seemingly a cross between that of a scientist scrutinizing a new species of bug and one of a lioness preparing for a kill.

"I said it's not a real ship," the woman repeated, her piercing black eyes zeroing in on Hayley's face. "Look there, below your foot."

"I —" Hayley looked down, as she was told, finally dropping her air-borne toes onto the foliage. She could not bring herself to speak.

"Come on, now. What do you have to say for yourself?" The woman did not sound amused.

"Yes, I know. It's a tree," Hayley said stupidly. *Oh... Did those words really just come out of my mouth? How idiotic can I be?* She could think of nothing else to say.

"So it is. It *is* a tree. My tree." Penetrating black eyes flickered. The woman was playing with her and seemed to be enjoying it. "Do you mind telling me exactly what you were doing *in* it?"

"I'm Hayley Buckman. You know...the new intern? I, uh...was just coming into the garden when I heard you...." Hayley paused. "That is — I mean, I was trying to go back, but then you came out, and I thought —"

"You thought you'd look foolish if you were caught eavesdropping, is that it?"

"Y-yes."

"Hmm. I see." The woman stepped closer and scanned Hayley from head to toe, as if making some kind of assessment. Two thin, gray arches rose high on her brow. "Ironic," she pointed out bitingly. "Isn't it?"

Hayley swallowed hard. "Quite." She waited while the woman continued her appraisal, instinctively knowing that any other action would be considered rude. Finally the woman turned away.

"All right, then," she said, waving one arm impatiently. "Come down out of there before a bird tries to nest on you."

Relieved, Hayley started to laugh before she realized that the comment was meant as an admonition and not a joke.

"I suppose I should be grateful you were able to identify that ship as a tree, considering the fact that you are our new intern," Theadora said disapprovingly.

Hayley choked back her laughter while trying to determine what was the correct response. If she agreed, she would sound self-deprecating; if she were to disagree, she would most likely be considered argumentative.

"I'm...so sorry about this." She tried to regain her composure. "And terribly embarrassed. Please be assured, climbing up into trees — when I'm not pruning them — is not an example of my normal behavior." Hayley spoke with a confidence and grace she did not feel.

"Really?" The woman sounded doubtful. "Tell me, is *eavesdropping* an example of your normal behavior?" The look in her eyes was triumphant.

Hayley lowered her head in shame. "No. I promise it is not, although that may not be easy for you to believe." The confidence was fading.

"Do not presume to tell me my mind!" Hayley jumped at the animosity in the woman's voice. "I've had quite enough of that today, I assure you." She continued on over Hayley's protest, "I don't know how your mother raised you, but here at

Newhaven, I am in charge. I demand to be treated with respect. Is that understood?"

Hayley nodded silently, stung by the reference to her mother.

"Very well," Theadora lowered her voice, sounding slightly mollified. "Then I should not expect any further *sneaky* behavior?"

"Certainly not." A hint of pride crept into Hayley's voice, but she refrained from arguing.

"All right, then." Theadora seemed to be weighing the next course of action. "I've sent Gabriel off to prune the roses —" Instinctively, Hayley glanced back over her shoulder, toward the terrace. "No! Not there," the woman scolded impatiently. "At the gardens, there...beyond the churchyard and cemetery." She pointed past the circle of yews, toward the opposite, northeast corner of the square. "I want you to go help him. You *can* prune roses?"

Hayley could not help herself. "It's as easy as sailing a ship," she quipped, instantly regretting it. For a moment, something flickered in Theadora's eyes, and she looked ready to order Hayley out of her sight. Then, apparently thinking better of it, she turned her back on the younger woman and marched away, without a word of farewell.

If the meeting could have gone any worse, Hayley could not have imagined how. Brushing a few stray twigs off her tan cotton pants, she dismally pointed herself in the direction Theadora had indicated, all thoughts of the previous shouting match pushed from her mind by thoughts of her own, more pressing, humiliation.

Eight

❧

Ah, bitter chill it was!
The owl, for all his feathers, was a-cold.
James Keats, *The Eve of St. Agnes*

Tucked amongst the mass of greenery, the faded blue T-shirt might have been taken for a flower, if it were not for the awkward mass of body and limbs to which it was attached. Hearing Hayley approach, Gabriel raised his head and grinned.

As Theadora had indicated, the stretch of land beyond the formal garden was home to yet another well-planned plot of greenery. No full blooms were yet in sight in the rose garden; several bushes were just starting to bud. But when they did blossom, Hayley guessed, no other beauty would be able to rival the glory of fragrance and color.

For the time being, however, the large shrubs were generally bare, except for a few sprouting leaves. To the untrained eye, they might even have appeared dead. Feeding this perception was the pile of dry cane that had already accumulated at the end of one long row.

"Hi, there, kiddo!" Hayley greeted Gabriel. "I'm here to lend a hand. Are you using those shears?"

"Help yourself," he offered cheerfully. Dressed in a T-shirt and shorts, he was clad in an outfit almost identical to the one he had worn the day before. "I was expecting Carson, but he hasn't shown up yet. There's gloves there, too. A bit large, I should think. But I expect they'll do."

Hayley slipped her tiny hands into the massive leather fingers, checked the blades of her pruning instrument, and settled herself on the opposite side of the bush Gabe was working on.

"You're doing a great job," she said, noting the attention he had given to his work. "How long have you been at it?"

"Oh, not beyond half an hour," Gabriel guessed. "Since seven, I think."

"My goodness! You'll make me look like a slacker," she teased.

"Don't worry, you'll get your chance," the boy warned. "Carson'll give you a few days to settle in. But then the taskmaster in him will take over, and he'll be giving you alarm calls at first light, just like he does me."

Hayley made a face. "I wish him luck. I've never been an early riser. At least not a *cheerful* one. Although the way things are going, I'm not about to put up a fight." She gave one dead branch a vicious snip.

"Beastly morning?" Gabe queried sympathetically.

"The worst." Grateful for the opportunity to vent, Hayley gave the boy a sketchy outline of the morning's events.

Gabriel sat back on his heels and, as she finished, let out a great roar of laughter.

"So you were caught out, eh? That's ripping! I suppose she got her wind up?"

Hayley nodded morosely.

"That's all right," he went on. "I've never known anyone to score off Theadora. I'm surprised she didn't threaten to send you packing."

"Well...she looked like she wanted to."

The boy shrugged. "I wouldn't worry about it. You're still here. She's hardly likely to sack you now. Especially with Francine gone."

Hayley seized the opening. "Tell me about her. Francine, I mean."

Gabe looked mildly surprised at her interest. "Francie? Oh, she was a smashing girl! Of course, we hardly got to know her before she'd off and gone."

"Why did she, do you think?" Hayley kept her voice light, like that of one making casual conversation.

The boy gave her a sly look. "Perhaps Theadora found her doing mime in the vegetable garden?" he offered wickedly.

A clump of dirt flew across the rose bush, striking the bridge of his nose. "Ha, ha." Hayley deadpanned. "You're killing me." Gabe grinned idiotically, looking thoroughly unrepentant. "I'm *serious*. Do you think Theadora might have fired her? Everyone seems to think it's a big mystery."

Gabriel concentrated on the thorny branches under his hands. "Well, there's no telling now. Francine's gone...and Theadora will never come clean."

Hayley eyed him curiously. "You don't like her either, do you?" she questioned, without qualifiying who "either" referred to.

The boy did not question it. For a moment, he seemed ready to speak, then caught himself. After a brief pause, he confessed, "Not especially. But my mom always said, 'if you can't say something nice....'"

Hayley laughed. "I know, I know. 'Don't say anything at all.' My mother told me the same thing. She was full of good advice. Like: 'Better to remain silent and be thought a fool than to speak out and remove all doubt.' Or something like that."

"Makes sense," Gabe allowed.

"So it does. Too bad I never listened." Hayley sighed. "I barely paid attention at the time. Now I wish she was still here to give me advice."

Deep green eyes searched her face. "Your mom's gone?" The young boy was back.

Hayley nodded wordlessly.

"Mine, too," he said matter-of-factly.

She nodded again. There was nothing else to say. For several minutes, they worked side-by-side, each lost in memories of a loving mother. Hayley reflected on the way her mom had worked with her as a child, teaching her which plants could be cultivated and which were simply weeds. Hayley wondered if Gabe's mom, too, had instilled in her children a deeply-felt love for all growing things. More likely, their interest had come from their father; the older Elliott had once been head gardener. As Hayley considered the bowed head before her, Carson's words resurfaced in her mind: *"He's been hardly any trouble; Mother raised him well...."* Obviously, Gabriel was trying to hold his tongue and behave honorably. But, to her shame, Hayley could not let the subject drop.

"It's not just Theadora, is it?" Then, in response to Gabe's raised eyebrow, "Oh, I'm not trying to pry!" she lied, throwing a dead stick into the pile of cuttings. "Don't say anything if you don't want to. It just seems odd, that's all. That episode in the gardens yesterday, between you two and Evan. Naturally, I'm feeling a bit curious…and nervous," she admitted, trying to defend herself.

Gabriel stopped his work and leaned forward slightly, his laughing eyes now somber. "You're serious?"

"Yes. I am." The earnest look on Hayley's face assured him that it was true.

"All right, then. I'll tell you this." Gabe's expression was grim; for a moment he looked almost exactly like his brother, rather than the carefree teenager Hayley had come to know. "Those Harringtons aren't to be trusted, that's all. Just watch yourself, Hayley. Trust no one. Especially not that big pot Evan. He's a ruddy liar." He snipped a branch angrily and moved on to the next barbed shrub. "Be careful."

She scowled. "'Be careful' as in 'watch your mouth or you'll get thrown out of here' or 'be careful' as in 'watch your back or you might wind up dead'?" Hayley knew she was being melodramatic, but Gabriel's warning had seriously unnerved her.

The boy looked around nervously. "Just be careful. That's all."

"Oh, Gabe," Hayley protested, waving her shears in the air. "I was just kidding. Surely you can't possibly think I could be in any real danger."

"I never said that." He glanced over her shoulder and brightened considerably. "Look! Here comes Carson." Hayley turned and saw the elder Elliott in the distance, cutting across the graveyard which lay between the church and rose gardens. Gabriel started clipping more furiously. "Let's hurry. I want to finish this row."

"Whoa, there!" Hayley watched as shears and rose stems flew. "Don't get sloppy now!" She considered the look of single-minded determination on Gabriel's face. "This isn't a race, you know."

"I know." He did not even look up. "I just don't want him to be disappointed."

"In you?" Hayley gave a snort of derision. "Hardly! I've seen the looks he gives you — like a proud papa with his first-born son." Too late, she realized she might be treading on dangerous ground, but Gabe kept right on working, seemingly unconcerned.

"I guess so. But...things have been tough for Cars lately."

"Tough how?"

"Just...personal stuff. You know." Hayley didn't know. But Gabriel did not appear ready to tell her. "On top of everything else," he lowered his voice, "he's smitten."

"Smitten?" It took Hayley a moment to digest the information. "With wh — Oh!" It all made sense. *"Our dear Francine...."* Suddenly, she felt out of sorts again. *If he liked the girl, he could have just said so.* Another snatch of conversation came back to her: *"Perhaps she had a secret boyfriend." "I'm sure matters will be very different for you."* Hayley concentrated on the green shoot under her hand, resisting the overwhelming urge to turn and glare at the man. "Was she...a very good gardener, this girl he's smitten with?"

Gabriel lifted his shoulders in a characteristic Elliott shrug. "Not enough time to tell, I'd say. But I rather think so." His green eyes danced.

"Huh. Well, why didn't he — Ow!" She winced as a large thorn pierced her protective glove. Pulling her hand from the heavy leather, she popped the afflicted thumb into her mouth and mumbled around it, "Ih he liched her sho much, why didn'd he do anyshing aboud id?"

"Probably because of our sist — Hey, Cars!" The boy jumped up at his brother's arrival and indicated the progress he'd made. "What do you think, brother? Smashing, eh?"

Sister? Hayley felt a tug of curiosity, but pride would not allow her to initiate a conversation with the new arrival. He stood before her in his long-sleeved, pine-green work shirt and earth-colored trousers and proudly surveyed the young man's handiwork. "Well done, I'd say. And Miss Buck — er, Hayley? How are you getting on?"

She nodded coolly at the bush in front of her. "You tell me."

The man knelt down obligingly and peered at the clipped branches. "Jolly good here, too. All right, you two, since you're so clever...." One side of his mouth curled upward in an endearing, lop-sided grin. "Tell me, what are the key elements of pruning?"

Oh, my word. It's a pop quiz! Hayley didn't know whether to laugh or be insulted. But considering the morning she'd had, she was still in no position to argue.

"Well, first, you make sure your pruning shears are sharp," Hayley offered. "It's critical that a clean cut be made. You don't want to crush the cane or the stem."

"Good. What angle do you cut at, Gabe?"

"Three hundred and sixty?" the boy offered, then smirked. "Kidding. Forty-five, of course."

"Right. And Hayley, where do you make the cut?"

"Just above, or as close as possible to, the swollen spot right above the scar where a leaf stem has fallen off — er, the bud eye."

"Quite. What about diseased or dead wood?"

Hayley was enjoying this now. *If only the game shows back home had such easy questions. I'd be a millionaire by now.* She pictured herself behind a bank of glowing lights. *"I'll take 'Aphids,' Alex, for four hundred."* To Carson, she reasoned, "You want to cut off dead wood as soon as possible, all the way back to the healthy wood."

"How do you know it's healthy?"

"Keep cutting until you reach a place where the pith in the center of the stem is white, not discolored."

"And how do you ensure that a bush grows outward?"

"Cut back only to an eye that is on the outward side of a stem. It keeps the canes from growing through the center of the bush."

Carson looked pleased. "Very good! All right, then. You're certainly qualified for the job. Hayley, I'd like you to keep on working out here. Gabe, why don't you come with me? I could use a hand pulling the mulch away from the perennial beds."

Gabe seemed undaunted by the prospect of the messy job. "Guess you're on your own, Hayley," he said, climbing out of the rose bed. "And *try to stay out of trouble,*" he admonished, stepping over her. The caution sounded out of place, coming from one so young.

"Trouble? What's this?" Carson looked from one to the other, sounding concerned.

"Oh, it's nothing," Gabe explained. "Hayley dropped a

brick this morning, and now she thinks she's getting the elbow."

Hayley blinked. The Britishisms were unfamiliar, but as far as she could tell, Gabriel had accurately communicated her plight.

"Oh, really?" Carson didn't look surprised, nor did he ask for an explanation. "Well, not to worry. If Theadora tries to pull something, she'll *not* get away with it." He smiled at Hayley. "We'll be back in awhile to check on you. Feel free to take a lunch break if we're not back by noon. See you then?" He turned to follow his energetic young brother, who was already twenty feet ahead.

Unable to speak, Hayley simply stared at his retreating back. For in a flash of realization, she had figured out the identity of the person who had been locked in confrontation with Theadora earlier that morning.

"Whatever it is, you're not *going to get away with it...."* If one allowed for the element of anger, the voices were a perfect match.

Under the slow-rising sun, the fleece-lined jersey should have provided sufficient warmth.

But suddenly, Hayley felt very, very chilled.

Nine

❦

His morning walk was beneath the elms in the churchyard;
"for death," he said, "he had been his next-door neighbour
for so many years, that he had no apology for dropping the
acquaintance."
Sir Walter Scott, *A Legend of Montrose*

H ayley rubbed one dirt-encrusted glove along the muscles of her neck, leaving a well-defined trail of chalky soil.

Already, it was a quarter past noon, and as yet, she had received no sign that Gabriel or his brother planned to return any time soon. Motivated by the murmurings of her stomach, which were quickly on their way to becoming full-fledged howls, Hayley made up her mind to venture back indoors to search out a mid-day meal.

She gathered up her tools and trimmings into several neat piles and glanced over her shoulder toward the chapel and churchyard, which lay between her and the main road. Spurred on by curiosity, or a desire to stretch her aching muscles, she decided to take an alternate route back to the house and pointed herself in the direction of the modest-sized cemetery.

A low, stone half-wall surrounded the burial site, symbolically, if not physically, separating the grave sites from the rest of the estate. In this section of the property, she noticed, no special effort had been made to beautify the grounds. Although the lawn was neatly trimmed, it was also marked by a number of wild weeds and scattered patches of crabgrass. In a place largely dominated by gardens, no flowers adorned the gravestones. The effect was strangely reassuring. It was, Hayley imagined, as if a sign were posted, which read: "Nothing to see here. Go on, folks — back to the gardens." She liked to think that this was a place where the dead could rest in peace.

Except...long-buried theology broke through to the surface of her mind. Hayley had always believed that physical surroundings had no impact on a person's after-life experiences. Once a person died, she was sure, his or her soul left the earth. She was taught that only those who believed in God and his Son would live in paradise; she tried not to think where the others must go. As was her habit when missing her parents, Hayley reminded herself that both were committed, heart and soul, to God. There was no doubt in her mind that they were in heaven, peacefully resting...or dancing, or laughing, or singing, or gardening.... She continued her walk, feeling somewhat comforted.

But something else nagged at her subconscious.... Hayley generally tried her best to ignore feelings of restlessness. With increasing frequency, she had been plagued by doubts that struck her at odd moments, but were especially difficult to deal with late at night. In the solemn setting of the churchyard, surrounded by souls long gone, the question became clearer.

What's going to happen when I *die?*

The rush of feelings that followed were unmistakably those of dread. Theoretically, Hayley argued silently, she should have nothing to worry about. As a child in Sunday school, she had knelt before kind-hearted Mrs. Shaw and pledged to follow

Christ. From that point on, she was an enthusiastic church-goer. Her parents encouraged her involvement, and she spent many evenings participating in church-sponsored youth events. Never once during that time had her commitment wavered.

It was after high school that things started to change. The transformation began innocently enough; with her intense study load, she barely had enough time to *sleep*, let alone go to church. When her parents asked her which congregation she was attending, she put them off, promising to get involved "next semester." After the first couple of years, they finally stopped asking. Hayley realized at the time that they were disappointed in her. But apparently they decided that their relentless questioning would do more damage than good, for they had finally stopped questioning and had left her alone to make her own choices.

They left me alone, *all right....* After the house fire, Hayley hadn't seen any point in going back to church. The final straw came when someone at their funeral, tried to comfort her: "We may not understand it, Hayley, but it had to be God's will."

That was enough to scare her away from church for good. *That* was the one thing that had always bothered her: church people always had a slick answer. Whenever something terrible happened — even something a person had *caused* to happen, through negligence or selfishness or even stupidity — the pat answer remained: "It was God's will."

Well, if that's how God's will works, Hayley figured, *I don't want to be a part of it.* It wasn't that she blamed God for her parents' deaths, exactly...although a part of her did accept blame. She suspected that their deaths had been some sort of retribution for the fact that Hayley had quit church. But even during those times when she felt inclined to give God the benefit of the doubt, she had to wonder: If God couldn't have prevented her parents' deaths, then what was the point in going to him with needs that were even smaller? Obviously, God expected her to make it on her own. And that's what she was doing. She was surviving. She was in control.

Carefully, Hayley stepped around and between the numerous, thick headstones, letting her eye drift over the inscriptions: Here Lyeth the Body of Elizabeth Raynes Harrington, Much Loved — Too Soon Departed, The 14th of March 1756....

"Too Soon Departed...." The cry of a devoted husband, crushed by the anguish of permanent separation. Hayley stood beside the marker, her fingers digging into the gravestone, as she felt the sense of bitter loss overwhelm and crush her spirit.

"I say, Miss.... Are you well?"

Hayley jumped up, startled, and found herself staring into a pair of hazy blue eyes, yellowed by age. They were set into a deeply lined face which belonged to a short, squat man she had never seen before. His hair was white and neatly trimmed, his clothes a heavy black, and it appeared from the way he stood that the man suffered from a slight hunch to his spine.

"I'm genuinely sorry," he apologized timidly. A look of regret flitted across his small, pointy features. "I've frightened you, haven't I?"

"No-o...." Frightened wasn't exactly the right word. Though odd-looking, the man appeared harmless. "I was just...thinking, that's all," she admitted sheepishly, brushing dusty hands against her trousers. "I'm afraid you caught me off guard."

"I see." The man noted her position at the gravestone, then looked back at her small face, which she was sure had gone chalky white. His bushy eyebrows furrowed. "I hope you don't mind me saying, but you look a bit peaky. Would you like to rest?" He waved a skinny arm, indicating the nearby chapel.

"Oh, no. I'm —" Hayley stopped as a look of unmistakable disappointment fell over the older man's eyes. "Well, now that I think of it — actually, yes, that would be lovely."

The diminutive man beamed. "Capital! Come along then." He turned and trudged in the direction of the church, all concern for Hayley's health forgotten in his delight at having a guest. Hayley followed, amusement pushing away all former thoughts of gloom. That the man was the reverend of Newhaven Chapel was obvious; what he wanted of her remained unclear. As it was clearly not designed for the purpose of entertaining visitors, the graveyard had no formal walkway. She stepped awkwardly over the markers as she hurried to catch up with the quickly-moving curate.

"Have you been inside the chapel?" the man asked eagerly as she joined him at his side.

"No. No, I haven't," Hayley admitted. "I just arrived yesterday, you see."

"Quite so." He nodded furiously and scurried up to the chapel doors. For a moment, Hayley paused, remembering the last time she was inside a church: her parents' funeral. "Come on, come on!" the man called to her, impatiently. Obediently, she placed her foot upon the flagstone.

Once inside, Hayley's hazy feelings of apprehension immediately dispersed. As a former architecture student, she felt like a child on Christmas morning. Her eyes danced over the English Gothic Perpendicular screen, the elaborately carved fourteenth-century baptismal font, and rows of windows made from brightly-colored stained glass. Overhead, eighteenth-century Dutch brass chandeliers hung from the high, vaulted ceiling, and behind the font was a fascinating relief of The Last Judgment. The surrounding walls were painted with colorful arms and crests which Hayley assumed to be those of the Harrington family.

"Please, take a pew," the man offered awkwardly, as if suddenly remembering that he was playing host. Hayley did as she was asked. "I have not even introduced myself. Reverend Rupert Archer," he said, sounding as if she might know what that meant. "And now, my dear," he began gently, "please do tell me…are you in need of help?"

"My word, no!" Hayley jumped off her pew, suddenly realizing that the man saw her as one of his 'lambs.' *That's what I get for being nice….* "I'm working up at the gardens with the Elliotts. I'd just stopped for a break, and I was thinking of home, feeling blue —"

The man did not appear convinced. "Come, now. Surely there was more to it than that?"

Hayley did not know what to say. The last thing she wanted was to share her life story with a complete stranger, no matter how honorable his intentions.

"Come now, take a chair," he coaxed. Hayley complied, seating herself nervously on the very edge of the wooden bench. "It is not my intention to pry," he continued. "But as a reverend, I'm not just a teacher of God's Word; I'm a student of human nature. I could tell you were in great distress, my dear." The old eyes were kind. "I don't know if there's anything I can do to ease your burden, but I do want you to know that whatever your trouble, God cares. And I care."

The words were simple, but they touched a chord in Hayley's heart. "I — really don't think there *is* anything you can do," she heard herself saying. "I've just been a little emotional since the death of my parents. That's normal isn't it? I'm afraid I get a little misty at the most awkward times."

"Such as this one?"

To her dismay, Hayley felt her lower lip tremble. She nodded helplessly, unable to find her voice. *Stop it, Hayley. Get control.*

"Would it be all right if I were to pray for you?" Reverend Archer offered. He took Hayley's sad-eyed silence to be affirmation and began: "Oh, Lord, have mercy on this your child. Touch her heart, and mend her wounds. Give her the wisdom to seek you and the courage to trust you. Help her to know that she needs you, and that she is precious in your eyes. In the name of the Father, and of the Son, and of the Holy Ghost, Amen."

With her jersey sleeve, Hayley wiped away the tears which threatened to spill. She couldn't remember the last time someone had prayed for her; she hardly remembered the last time she *herself* had prayed, other than a passing, "Help me, Lord"— a practice which had become for her the mental equivalent of rubbing a rabbit's foot and had received from her about as much emotional investment.

The man was looking at her, waiting.

"Uh..." Hayley looked around, trying to think of an escape. "Thanks ever so much. It's been a long — that is..." She stopped and met his look of compassion. "Really." She smiled suddenly: a tiny, wavering smile, but the emotion was genuine. "That was very kind of you. It might have been just what I needed."

Reverend Archer nodded confidently but did not push her response.

"Thank you, too, for showing me the church." Hayley stood. "It really *is* lovely."

The man's face glowed with pride, assuming the role of proud host once more. "Please come — any time. I, myself, enjoy walking in the churchyard each morning. It's been my practice for so many years, the chaps out there," he nodded toward the graveyard, "have become like old friends." He laughed self-consciously. "I suppose you think that's odd? But I couldn't break the habit now if I tried. Of course," he said brightly, "it served me well this morning, for it brought me to you. Isn't that so?"

A look of tenderness touched Hayley's face. She reached out and patted his hand kindly. "Yes, that's so."

"Well…" Reverend Archer groaned as he rose from the pew and followed her to the chapel door. "…you know where to find me, my dear, if you need me. I'm off at the Green quite often during the week, visiting my flock." He raised his eyebrows for emphasis. "But God is always here."

For a split-second, Hayley almost giggled, the cynic in her rising to the surface once more. The man sounded so solemn; his choice of phrasing *so* melodramatic! But it was clear that he meant every word, and she forced herself to focus on his sincerity.

"Thank you for the reminder," she said simply and turned away.

"Think about what I said!" the reverend called after her. "Don't forget!"

Hayley nodded and waved, then resumed her walk toward

the house while doing exactly that: reflecting upon the reverend's words. So absorbed was she by her thoughts, that it seemed mere seconds before the floral parterres were once again in sight and the house in full view. In the distance, she spied a figure, waving cheerfully. Seeing her approach, the person settled lazily against the garden wall, to wait. As she drew closer, the man's features seemed to take form, and Hayley realized that it was Evan, looking dapper in a ribbed crewneck sweater and pleated linen pants, both of a rich, dark mocha. Her heart leapt as she remembered her resolve from the night before.

"Ah, Hayley," he purred. "Well met. How are you getting on this afternoon?"

"Fine thanks." Unconsciously, one hand flew to her damp eyes as she tried to rub away any make-up smudges. "A bit stiff from working in the rose gardens. And *starved.*"

"Now that's a bit of luck!" Evan looked pleased. "I'd just come to invite you on a picnic. Simon, Isabelle, and I were going to walk down to the lower gardens with a basket. Won't you join us?"

"Oh, I don't know Evan…." Hayley hated to be rude, but the prospect of spending an hour fending off Evan's advances and ignoring Isabelle's rude stares hardly seemed appealing. "It seems I'm working today, and I'm not done in the rose garden —"

"Nonsense!" Evan interrupted. Taking Hayley's arm, he tucked it into the crook of his own and began leading her toward the house. "You have to eat sometime. This isn't a prison, you know, whatever Elliott would have you believe."

"But —" Hayley protested, trying to pull away.

"I'm serious," Evan insisted. "Besides, you said you're hungry, and I'm afraid it's too late to get anything in the kitchen. Theadora's eaten, and no one knew where you were," he chided. "You'll have to wait now until tea, unless you come with us," he finished triumphantly.

"Oh, all *right*," Hayley agreed, but pulled her arm away in irritation. "But I do need to be back within an hour. Have you seen Carson?" She glanced around anxiously.

"Don't worry about Elliott," Evan scoffed. "If he gives you any back chat, I'll give him a dressing down."

Hayley rolled her eyes, but Harrington was so caught up in his own thoughts, he did not even notice. The man was certainly used to getting his own way. *Is that what Gabe was warning me about?* Was Evan the harmless playboy he seemed, or something more threatening? The answer wasn't clear. Hayley knew only one thing for sure. Charming or not, Evan Harrington was beginning to get on her nerves.

en

Keep yourself to yourself.
Charles Dickens, *Pickwick Papers*

Flanked by the two dark-haired Harringtons and trailed by a sulking Isabelle, Hayley made her way down the charming, daffodil-lined path which led across the terraced lawn and to the lower gardens.

"Where were you before I found you?" Evan asked, casually tucking one hand into a trouser pocket. "You said something about the rose garden, but I was just there, and I didn't see you anywhere."

"Oh — that," Hayley hedged. "I was just...exploring a bit."

"Exploring? *Do* tell." Simon sounded mildly interested. He shifted the large picnic basket from one arm to the next. "Where were you poking about?"

"Actually, I was taking the long route back to the house, through the churchyard," Hayley admitted, "when I ran into Reverend Archer."

"Oh, him!" Evan let out his breath in an expression of disgust. "That silly old gaffer. I suppose he started rattling on about a bunch of spiritual nonsense."

Simon gave him a look of warning. "Now, brother —"

"What? You know what I think! He's a patsy."

His younger brother looked nervous. "Don't be cocky, Evan."

"Come on, mate. Don't tell me you're *still* afraid of him?" He gave Hayley a sly grin. "Brother has always thought the reverend had the power to call down God's wrath upon him."

Hayley blinked and looked from one man to the next. "Well, I don't know if that's true. But I don't think it's right to make fun of the church or a man of God," she said irritably.

Evan stopped in the path. "You scatty thing!" He looked amazed. "You're afraid of him, too!"

"No, I'm not!" Hayley glared at him and kept walking. "As a matter of fact, I *liked* him. He was…very nice to me."

"Well, of course he was!" Evan sputtered, rushing to catch up. "I'm sure he imagined you to be one of his blind followers. Let me guess, was 'God loves you' the first thing to pop out of his mouth or the second?"

Hayley pushed forward without giving him another glance. The man knew too much by half. "I'll have you know he asked about *me,* thank you very much And my welfare."

"And *then* he started rattling on about God's love. Isn't that so?" He watched her expectantly.

"Oh, all *right!*" Hayley exploded and turned on her heel. Beside and behind her, Simon and Isabelle came to an abrupt halt. "He talked about God's love. There. Are you happy? What do you expect? He's a *reverend* for pity's sake!"

Evan led the party forward again, wearing a self-satisfied grin. "I know that. I just hate all the church talk. 'God loves you,' and 'Peace be with you,' and all that. It's all a bunch of rot, if you ask me — nothing but empty words."

Hayley stared glumly at her shoes as she followed. She understood what Evan was complaining about; she'd given nearly the same argument when confronted by church-going friends back home. But coming from this cocky stranger, the line of reasoning sounded presumptuous and cold.

"It's all about power if you ask me," Evan was saying. "The C. of E. —" He broke off and glanced at Hayley. "That is, the Church of England takes care of its own. All right, so he's at a proprietary chapel, which means Theadora has him in her pocket. But hark at what the old gaffer's got: he gets the living of the parish — not just a home, but a rural pocket living. Not to mention that he has those townsfolk who still go to church eating out of his hand. He has your number now, though, Hayley," he warned, "you'll have to keep away from the church yard if you want to avoid the dreary old git —"

"Leave her alone, Evan," Simon muttered, looking uncomfortable.

"All right, you jelly babies." The older Harrington laughed. "I'll leave your religion alone. Hullo! I see a fine spot…there, just ahead. Coming, Issy?"

As Evan and Simon moved to set up the blanket and lunch basket upon the lush, green grass, Isabelle stole silently to Hayley's side. "Keep yourself away from Simon," she hissed quietly, and without a word of explanation, she slunk back to the side of her fiancé.

Hayley remained motionless for several minutes, frozen by shock. Not knowing what else she could do, she at last settled on taking a place on the blanket beside Evan and concentrating on two simple goals: keep a smile on your face, and get through lunch as quickly as possible.

Irritation gave way to undiluted pleasure as Hayley bit into a light, crisp Albany biscuit, spread with a thick layer of fresh kipper paté.

"My goodness!" she exclaimed, swallowing a mouth-watering biteful. "This is incredible. Do you eat like this every day?" Her eyes surveyed the small banquet spread on the blanket before her: thick crusts of French bread with slices of roast beef, tomato, and lettuce; generous wedges of cheese; an enormous jar of pickles; and tea.

"Oh, no," Evan demurred, helping himself to the smoked herring. Stretched lazily across the soft wool fabric, he was the very picture of indolence. "Usually, we lunch on hot savories. But as we were eating out in the garden today, I asked Cook to serve something that could be taken out of doors."

"Really?" Hayley said curiously. She turned to check on Simon and Isabelle, who were engaged in an intense conversation perhaps a hundred yards away. Against a brightly-colored bed of columbine, primroses, and cowslip, their dark clothing — his, a charcoal fleece V-neck, hers, a navy sun dress — gave them the appearance of being mere shadows. Hayley turned back to Evan. "How interesting. I would think that since it didn't need to be kept hot, I might have taken my own lunch up at the house," she accused.

"Ah, I've been caught out!" Evan smiled shamelessly. "Don't be angry, Hayley. So I kept you from lunching alone. Where's the harm?" He exhibited no doubt in her willingness to forgive.

"The *harm*, Evan, is that you take too much for granted," she chided, feelings of displeasure resurfacing. "You've got to stop this...this —"

"All right, all right," he interrupted, laughing easily. "I've strong-armed you, haven't I? I take your point. I shan't push any longer."

"See?" Hayley grumbled. "There you go again, interrupting. You don't *listen* very well, Evan."

The laughter stopped. His eyes flashed like sparks off steel. "I'm sure I *do* listen, my dear," he responded, his warm tone cooling slightly. "I can see you've got your wind up. But look — it's a cracking fine day. Don't let's spoil it." Evan glanced toward Simon and Isabelle, whose voices were now raised in conflict. "Don't be acid. It's only," he glanced at his watch, "five and twenty past one. Finish your lunch and I'll see you back to your post straightaway." He flashed a melting smile obviously intended to thaw the chilling of her heart.

"All right," Hayley agreed, trying to keep her voice light. This man was related to her employer; she could not afford to offend. "But Evan, you must know...I'm here to work, not to play." Although his behavior that day had reinforced the wisdom of her decision, Hayley still felt uncomfortable following through. She avoided his gaze, concentrating on the small piece of biscuit she was crumbling between thumb and forefinger. "I'm not your — date, you know. And I can't be. We need to keep our relationship professional." Hayley raised her face, her expression echoing the request. "Please."

Gray eyes clouded over in a chilling expression that reminded Hayley of an incoming storm. "I see." For once, Evan Harring-ton seemed at a loss for words. Silence hung heavily between them. "How foolish of me," he began icily. "I did not realize —"

"Evan —" Hayley broke in, trying to explain.

At that moment, Isabelle uttered a particularly loud

exclamation. Angrily, she pulled away from her fiancé and stormed back in the direction of the house.

"What was *that* about?" Evan asked dryly as his brother approached.

"Can't you guess?" Simon responded ruefully. Then, to Hayley, with a look of regret, "Please accept my most sincere apology. Isabelle — that is, we *both* have been terribly rude to you, our guest." He sighed heavily and seated himself on the blanket beside her. "I did not foresee there being a scene today. Unfortunately, my fiancée and I have some personal business we've been trying to work through, and we've been having rows at the most awkward times. I'm sorry it happened in your presence." He grimaced. "Twice."

"It's very unfortunate," Hayley sympathized. "She didn't have more than a few bites of her lunch." She followed Isabelle's retreat with her eyes.

"Shall I go after her, brother?" Evan offered unenthusiastically.

Simon hesitated, considering. "No…no need to bother. I've no intention of ruining *everyone's* lunch."

"That's quite all right," Evan responded, his voice flat. "I do believe I'm finished here. Isn't that right?" He stood and looked at Hayley pointedly.

She stared up at him, at a loss to know how she should respond. "If — that's what you'd like."

"Evan, *sit down.…*" Simon's voice had an edge to it, but Evan ignored him. Facing Hayley, he inclined his head, then he turned back to Simon. "Brother." With another stiff nod, he was off. Hayley watched him go.

"Again," Simon offered, remorsefully, as the man strode

away, "I'm forced to apologize. I'm afraid my brother has shark manners." Then, in response to Hayley's look, "Obviously you have foiled some plan of his. I suppose you refused his attentions?"

"We...just had a little disagreement, that's all," Hayley explained diplomatically.

"Well done!" Simon approved. "He's a bit highfed, our Evan. It's terrific that someone disagrees with him for a change."

"It's just that he's so — pushy!" she vented.

"I know. But Evan's quite a steady chap, under all the pomp," Simon assured her, lounging back against the blanket. "He just needs the right woman to get him to toe the line." He raised one eyebrow inquisitively.

"Well, whoever she is...I wish her luck." Hayley sounded doubtful. She gave Evan's retreating back one last glance, then turned to her companion. "I hope everything is all right with you and Isabelle? It wasn't — I mean, she wasn't worried about —" she stumbled, wishing to apologize for causing any dissension, yet not wanting to appear conceited.

The look Simon gave her was compassionate. "You're a sweet thing, aren't you? No, don't worry a bit." For the first time, Hayley noticed the deep wrinkles in his forehead, which made him look tense and exhausted. He rubbed a manicured hand against his brow. "It's an old argument, I'm afraid, and not one that's likely to be resolved any time soon." Hayley looked at him nervously. She had no desire to hear about his private affairs, but the man looked like he desperately needed someone in whom he could confide.

To her relief, he did not push the subject any further.

Instead, he asked, "How are you getting on so far? Has Theadora come down upon you yet? If not, just wait — she will!" The look he gave her was genuinely sympathetic.

Before she even realized what she was doing, Hayley had begun to share, once again, the story of her humiliation in the cypress. Unlike Gabriel, Simon did not laugh. Quite the opposite, he seemed somewhat concerned.

"I don't suppose…you know who she was arguing with?" he wondered aloud.

Hayley paused. Simon seemed like he could be trusted, but instinctively she felt an urge to withhold the gardener's name. "No," she lied. "I doubt it was anyone I've met. I didn't recognize the voice."

"Hmm. It all sounds quite…uncomfortable," he commiserated.

"*That's* an understatement." Hayley sighed. "What a way to start out my summer! It'll be weeks, if not months, before I'm able to look Theadora in the eye. That's assuming she even lets me stay."

Simon shared in her mood. "Summer is sure to be a disaster for me as well," he said gloomily, then finally broke down and said in a low voice, "Isabelle and I plan to marry this autumn. But things are not going well."

"I — see." One would be blind not to.

"It's not just simple jealousy," he confided. "*That* I could deal with — could even *understand* if this were a true marriage. But it's not."

"It's — not?" Hayley felt confused. In the United States, a fake marriage usually meant that someone was illegally helping another to get a green card. "Then what is it?"

"Actually, it's more of a business arrangement." Simon looked embarrassed.

Hayley sucked in her breath. "How awful!" she exclaimed before she could help herself.

"I know, I know what you're thinking," he began. "A person should marry for love, and all that. I always thought so, too. But — I'm thirty-two and I've not found anyone as of yet. And then, there's the family to consider."

"The family?" Hayley blinked, not understanding.

"That's right. You don't know, do you, how expensive it is to keep up an estate like this? We count on the trippers. That's why the gardens are so important. Money's been getting tighter every year. We can hardly go on like this forever."

"But —" Hayley did not want to know any more of the financial details. "What about Isabelle?"

"Oh, I'm fond of Issy — we all are," Simon said, picking at a biscuit. "But love? No, I don't think so. I've been honest with her all along. It was part of the agreement: the Chevalier money, the Harrington name and position. Up until recently, things were going smashingly. But in the last month or so, she's been having jealous fits. When we go into the city, she imagines I'm looking at every woman on the street. Can you imagine?" He chuckled ruefully. "I'm not my brother, Hayley. I'm no playboy. If I had found the right woman, I would have settled down long ago and been quite happy. As it is, I'm doing the best I can. I'm not trying to hurt anyone, truly I'm not," he said earnestly. The devastating Harrington eyes caught and held hers. "Please say you understand?"

"Well...I can't do that," Hayley objected. Something about his plea tugged at her heart strings. "Although I believe you really *don't* mean to hurt anyone. But be careful, won't you? Women's — *people's* hearts are fragile. Don't hurt Isabelle any more than you already have."

His gray eyes twinkled. "I was right. You *are* sweet. Now, if you only had a fortune...." He laughed and pulled her to her feet. "Come on. Let's catch up to the others and see if we can make a bit of peace."

However, peace was not to be made — at least, not that day. After lunch, Hayley went directly back to the rose gardens, escaping Evan's sullen mood and Isabelle's icy glares. Once or twice, Carson checked on her work, offering words of encouragement and bits of gardening advice, and Hayley managed to get a tea tray from the timid maid later that afternoon. Afterwards, she treated herself to a long, luxurious soak in the elegant, but extremely chilly, guest bath. Skipping high tea, she chose to retire to her room early in order to catch up on her reading and her sleep.

It was not until her hair was dried and combed, her knees and elbows slathered with lotion, and her feet tucked into warm, woolen slippers that she noticed the note.

It lay on top of her pillow, neatly folded, with the word 'Buckman' scrawled on the outside of the top flap. There was no envelope.

Curious, but not alarmed, Hayley reached for the slip of white parchment paper and unfolded it. At the top of the page, the initials T. H. were engraved in a great, swooping flourish.

The note was short, hand-scrawled, and read:

GO HOME

LEAVE WHAT ISN'T YOURS.

I KNOW WHAT YOU'RE ABOUT, AND YOU SHAN'T
GET AWAY WITH IT.

Hayley's hands began to tremble as a voice haunted her memory. *"Whatever it is, you're not going to get away with it...."*

Carson's words.

Theadora's paper.

Isabelle's attitude.

Someone wanted desperately for Hayley to leave Newhaven. The only question was...

Who?

Eleven

> *To be rude to him was courtesy.*
> Dante Alighieri, *Inferno*

"Now 'tis the spring, and weeds are shallow-rooted; suffer them now and they'll o'er grow the garden,'" Theadora quoted, waving one mud-covered glove in the air.

Hayley met Carson's eyes over a cluster of blue lungwort.

"She's waxing poetic," he informed her in a stage whisper.

"Have a care, Elliott!" Theadora warned from behind a two-foot mound of silver king artemisia. "I'll not have any back chat. You there!" She waved a handful of gray-green leaves at Hayley. "Ship girl. What was I just saying?"

Hayley raised her head from her weeding and blinked at the woman. "I beg your pardon?" She stopped and scratched one leg.

"Keep at it! I expect a proper day's work," Theadora ordered. Then, when Hayley had resumed her task, she insisted impatiently, "The *line*, girl. From which play does it come?"

"I'm sorry — I have no idea," Hayley confessed, carefully keeping her hands in the dirt.

"Uh-oh," Carson muttered without looking up.

Theadora caught a sharp breath. "Don't you people *read* in America? My word, it's *Shakespeare*. Queen Margaret in *Henry IV, Part II.*" She gave a snort of superiority.

Hayley kept digging, without feeling any sense of alarm. Over the past few days, she had decided that Theadora's grousing was actually a sort of a hobby, rather than an expression of actual displeasure. Since Hayley had arrived, she seemed to have become Theadora's prime target.

"All right then," the older woman continued. "You've been working in the borders for two days now. Tell me what you know about them."

"Let me see...." Hayley barely supressed a smile. It was easy to see where Carson's rose garden 'Pop Quiz' had originated. She recited, like an obedient child, a fair rendition of a textbook definition: "Herbaceous borders are among the highlights of the very best gardens in England. They represent a conscious effort to combine a wide variety of shapes and colors and are largely made of perennials — so they come back looking generally the same year after year. As opposed to —"

"All right," Theadora snapped. "I know that! I didn't ask what borders *were*, for goodness' sake. I asked you to tell me what you know *about* them."

"Well...." Hayley considered. "It's important to keep them well maintained, as we've been doing these past two days: deadheading and dividing the crowded plants. But if the majority of plants *are* perennials, like you have here, the border will naturally involve less work than a bed of annuals, simply in terms of planting time." She thought for a moment. "The borders should be mulched over winter. The gardener then pulls the mulch away in early to mid-spring, once the new shoots begin to sprout, and works the fertilizer into the soil, being careful not to damage the young plant roots."

Theadora looked somewhat satisfied. "What type of fertilizer should be used?"

"Compost, bonemeal, or an all-purpose fertilizer, like five-ten-five."

"Hm. If perennials are so easy to care for, why do we bother with annuals?"

"The variety extends the blooming season," Hayley explained dutifully. "And using different types of flowers just…adds more notes to the song." She blushed, expecting Theadora to laugh at the metaphor, but for once the woman held her tongue. "Now is the perfect time to divide the perennials that bloom in late spring, summer, and fall. They're prepared to grow fast this time of year — it's in their DNA, I suppose — so they bounce back pretty quickly."

Theadora could find nothing to argue with in Hayley's explanation, but still was not content. "How are borders planned?" she challenged.

"Hmm." Hayley kept digging while she thought. "Well, the taller plants go in the back, I know —"

"No," Theadora interrupted, giving Hayley a disparaging look. "I mean, how does one choose perennials for the bed?"

"I — don't know. I would imagine you just try to capture as many colors and varieties as possible."

The older woman looked at Hayley as if she were a simpleton. "I think not. Now, pay attention.…" She looked pleased to have found something to lord over Hayley. "One does not simply select two of everything, as if it were an ark." Theadora sniffed. "One may choose a color scheme — monochromatic, harmonious colors, contrasting colors, or polychromatic. Of course, our borders have been designed to be —"

"Polychromatic," Hayley supplied.

"Quite." Theadora appeared irritated by the interruption. "Or one may choose to design a garden around the foliage itself, rather than the plants' flowers — perhaps including only those with gray or silver leaves. One might build a garden around a particular plant family, or person, or historical time period —"

Hayley half-listened as her thoughts returned to the question which had occupied her thoughts for nearly three days.

Who was the person who wrote the note?

She had very nearly decided it was Isabelle. It had to be. Although Theadora's social skills were less than admirable, it was she who had brought Hayley to Newhaven in the first place. If the woman wanted to send Hayley away, all she had to do was dismiss her. Besides which, if she'd wanted to remain anonymous — as had the note's author — she would be foolish to use her own letterhead. Unless she *wanted* Hayley to discount her as a suspect, for exactly that reason. Perhaps Francine had received just such a note...?

Hayley's head was spinning. Such reasoning was just too complex to be believable. It was quite a stretch, even for her imaginative mind. Then, *Carson...?*

She smiled at the top of his familiar, weathered linen cap, which was bent over a patch of Jerusalem sage. As she'd worked with him closely, over a period of several days, Hayley had come to see him as a thoughtful, kind-hearted man. True, he had a tendency to talk big when one of the Harringtons pushed his buttons. But he was exceedingly kind. He had managed to return her rental car the day after her arrival, for which she would be forever grateful. The man also loved his work — and was good at it. He adored his brother. Who knew what else he cherished?

Francine. The thought triggered a profound sense of frustration. Hayley liked to think she and Carson were becoming friends. But in all the time they'd worked together, never once had he mentioned the girl with whom he was, as Gabe called it, "smitten." It was almost as if he had something to hide....

No. That line of reasoning was just as ridiculous as the first. The note had to be written by Isabelle. There simply wasn't any other possibility. The woman obviously was distraught — not to mention manner-deficient. No.... *As strange as the others might be, no one else could be so incredibly antisocial.*

"You there! Yes, you...the sneaky one."

Hayley groaned. *Then again....*

Theadora gave her a penetrating, black-eyed stare. "Tell me," she said, waving the trowel in her hand, "exactly how your interest in gardening came about."

In her shock, Hayley nearly dropped her hand fork. Never before had Theadora shown the slightest interest in her as anything other than an extension of her gardening arm. "Me? *My* interest?"

"Yes, you!" Theadora raised her eyes heavenward and lashed out at the plant before her. "Who else? Don't mimic; answer!"

"We-ll," Hayley paused. "I suppose it started with my mother. When I was a toddler, I remember, she used to take me exploring in the woods out behind our house. While we were on these 'nature walks,' she'd pick different leaves off the bushes and trees and put them in my little hands." She stared into one dirt-covered palm. "We'd take them home and spread them out on the big oak kitchen table…comparing the different sizes and colors and textures.…"

Hayley paused and followed with one finger the outline of an oval, lungwort leaf, spotted with white. "Then she would get out pieces of old, yellowed typing paper, and we'd lay them over the leaves and scribble over each one with a different-colored crayon.… The stems and veins would all trace through, we'd cut them out, and we'd have this *wonderful* collection of brightly-colored leaves." Glancing up, she was shaken from her reverie by the sight of her two co-laborers, who were watching her closely, their work tools idle. Carson's eyes were compassionate; Theadora's intense.

"I guess a love of nature just runs in the family," Hayley went on brightly, trying to downplay the moment. She began to dig again.

"I see," Theadora said indifferently. "I believe you mentioned in your application that your parents are dead."

"That's right." At the time, the question regarding family background had struck Hayley as odd; she had rebelliously answered with one single word: Orphaned.

"Theadora!" Carson objected loudly. "Show a little compassion, would you?"

Theadora ignored him and turned back to Hayley. "Tell me, was your mother a good woman?"

Hayley froze. "I don't take your meaning." Things were getting too personal. She turned to Carson, her eyes begging for rescue.

"That is," Theadora continued stiffly, "did she stress the importance of loyalty? Honor? Dedication to family?"

"Theadora!" Carson barked. His face slipped quickly into a mask of anger. "You're going too far. Leave her alone."

"This doesn't concern you!" the woman snapped, turning on him. "I'm merely finding out what sort of an individual I have living under my roof. I have every reason to believe this woman is an eavesdropper." Hayley turned pale. "I believe I have the right to inquire as to whether she has *any* family values at all," Theadora went on.

Carson drew himself to his full height and advanced upon his employer, stopping at a distance of about eight feet.

"I said, that's enough!" he repeated, looking grim. "You may intimidate everyone else around here, but you don't frighten me. And you will *not* badger Hayley."

Theadora stared back at him for a long, silent moment, her eyes flashing in anger. Finally, she bit out, "You have challenged me twice. The first time, I allowed it to pass. Today, I will do the same. *Do not test me a third time.* If you do so, you will be forced to leave Newhaven — and we both know that is not what you want...don't we?"

Green eyes clashed with black in a battle of wills before Theadora finally blinked and lowered her gaze. Without another word to Hayley, she threw down her gloves and trowel and stormed out of the garden, leaving broken dignity and scattered emotions in her wake.

Hayley turned her attention to a cluster of candytuft. "Thank you," she said quietly, her hands shaking against the small white flowers and narrow green leaves. "I'm afraid she really caught me off guard that time — and just when I'd begun to think she was all bark and no bite."

"It's all right," Carson assured her, his voice now gentle. He moved to Hayley's side. "She forgets herself sometimes. These Harringtons just need someone to stand up to them every now and then."

"You should be more careful, though," Hayley warned him, her eyes wide. "I've been here less than a week, and I've seen — or heard — you at odds with Evan once and Theadora twice."

"Theadora twice?" Carson looked surprised. "You hadn't seen me argue with Theadora until today."

"That's right," Hayley backpedaled. "I just — oh, look how befuddled she's got me! I can't even count straight. But that's not the point."

"It's not?" Carson smiled softly in the face of her confusion.

"*No*. It's not," she chided, moving on to the next plant. "The *point* is that you'll have to learn to control your temper, or you'll be out of a job."

Carson followed her. "Theadora wouldn't actually sack me," he argued. "She really *is* all bark, if you want to know the truth."

"I don't know…she sounded awfully serious. And what was that business about you not wanting to leave Newhaven? The way you've been getting on, I should think you'd be thrilled to leave. If I didn't need the credit, I'd be on the next bus out, myself."

Carson shrugged. "I suppose she thinks everyone should be thrilled and grateful for the opportunity to live and work in her presence. The Harrington ego and all."

"I suppose that's a cleverly-disguised reference to Evan?" Hayley teased.

"Ah! You recognized his description!" The gardener threw

up his arms in a gesture of victory.

"Carson! You'd better be careful. I can't believe how rude you were to him on the day I arrived."

"Oh, that?" Carson dropped his arms, looking unconcerned. "That was nothing. What I really wanted to do was —" He stopped himself. "There goes my temper. Let's just say that as far as Harrington goes, I was being polite."

"Well…I guess I can see why you'd feel that way —" Hayley started to confess.

"So you've caught on to his game?" Carson grinned. "You're more clever than I thought."

Hayley ignored the barb. "Laugh if you want to," she argued, pride keeping her from admitting that Carson had been completely right. "But he's been perfectly charming to me."

"Do tell," Carson murmured dryly. "So what are you doing out here with a damp squib like me?" he said offhand, dividing a section of columbine.

"Well…," Hayley pretended to consider. "You're a fairly *likable* squib, I'll give you that."

"More likable than that other rotter?" Carson prompted.

"Well…yes, I suppose." Hayley grinned at her friend.

"Or his bumbledon of a brother?"

"My word." Hayley laughed. "Where *do* you people come up with these expressions?"

Carson's gaze did not waver.

Her spirits lifted somewhat, Hayley decided to have a little fun. "Oh, I don't know…Simon seems nice enough," she teased.

Carson's face fell. "That's a joke, surely?"

"What do you mean?" Hayley feigned innocence. "I think he's a prince."

"A prince?" There was nothing make-believe about his irritation. "You are a silly little scrap!"

"What?" The smile fell from her face. "There's no need to call me names!"

"I cannot believe you would see the truth about one Harrington and be so blind about the other!" he fumed.

The joke had gotten out of hand, but Hayley was in no mood to apologize. "I don't see why you think I have to agree with you on everything, Carson. It's none of your business, anyway, *who* I like."

"Fine, then. Have it your way. I'm sorry I ever got involved."

Hayley's heart fell as he turned to go. He was her only friend at Newhaven, not counting Gabe; she couldn't afford to destroy the relationship. But he *was* being unreasonable — so domineering, so angry.

"By the way," he said coolly, turning. "I had something left for you in your room when you first arrived. You never said anything. Didn't you get it?"

Hayley stared at him. It couldn't be true....

"You? That was from *you?*"

"Yes, it was." He looked mildly surprised. "Hadn't you guessed?"

"Well, yes...the thought crossed my mind. But I thought — I didn't understand what it meant." Her face clouded over in dismay.

"I should have thought it was obvious," Carson said, his voice flat.

"Yes, I suppose it was." Hayley was still reeling from the shock. "I...had no idea you felt that way."

"Well, now you have, haven't you?"

"Yes." She fell silent.

"And?" he prodded.

"And—" The image of black letters on parchment danced in her mind's eye. *GO HOME....* She took a deep breath and began bravely, "I don't know what triggered that sentiment, Mr. Elliott, but...I wish you had not expressed it. Whatever your feelings are, they're your problem — not mine," she mumbled unhappily, accidentally crushing the stalk in her hand. "I'd appreciate it if you'd keep them to yourself in the future."

Carson stared at her, his face like stone. Then he shrugged and turned away.

Twelve

❧

"*Bid me love, and I will give/A loving heart to thee.*
Robert Herrick, *To Anthea, Who May Command Him Anything*

Hayley tugged at the drawstring of her heavy leather jacket, pulling the warm, faux fur hood more tightly around ears that were starting to numb.

Living up to its reputation, the English weather had been traditionally mild all week. But even in Britain, Hayley quickly realized, a late night stroll had the effect of intensifying one's response to the chill of spring.

Hayley's excursion had little purpose, other than to provide a moment of freedom from the house which had become unbearably suffocating. Two days had passed since Hayley's confrontation with Carson; since that time, she had spent nearly all of her time working, and dining, and reading alone in her room. *Carson, Isabelle, Theadora, Evan....* More people were furious with her than weren't; it seemed that the only friends she had left were Gabriel and Simon.

It doesn't matter what other people think, Hayley consoled herself, slopping her feet through a puddle. *It wasn't like any one of* them *was a particular prize....* Something about the analysis didn't ring true, but she pushed down the nagging doubt. Perhaps it was sour grapes thinking, but she needed all the emotional fortitude — real or imagined — she could muster.

From behind her, Hayley heard the crack of a twig, just beyond the garden wall. She turned. "Hello?"

Silence echoed back at her.

For a moment, Hayley hesitated. Then, smiling wryly, she continued on. Undoubtedly, the English countryside, like that of America, was filled with night marauders, such as foxes or raccoons. *No one will even speak to me during the day; I hardly think they'd venture after me at night.*

Hayley wandered aimlessly along the flower beds which consumed so much of her daily thoughts and energy. Passing the clipped cypress 'ship' which had caused her such embarrassment, she stepped within the ring of ancient yews. Midway into the circle, her eyes fell upon the large block of stone at the garden's center, which she'd noticed many times during the week but had never taken the time to carefully examine.

The pedestal was quite substantial, perhaps four feet in height, and widened at both the bottom and top. Into each side panel was etched the simple pattern of two perfect squares, one within the other. The piece had suffered a great deal of damage over the years; the base and sides were severely cracked, and at the top a deep, ugly indentation marked the stone, as if someone had hacked away at it with a blunt instrument. *What was it Evan said about a statue that was removed long ago?* Hayley bent to take a closer look, but there was no sign as to what the figure might have been, no inscription on the stone.

At that moment, a strange chill came over her. Her wide brown eyes scanned the garden nervously. If someone were actually there, Hayley knew, she would have little chance of seeing the figure first; the circle of yews provided a more than adequate screen for one wishing to avoid discovery.

It wasn't the first time that week she had felt someone was watching her, although she had never actually caught anyone doing so. At first, she had dismissed the feeling as paranoia, stemming from the week's unfortunate events. Later, she had attributed it to the possibility of Carson or Theadora observing her work from a distance.

Something squished against the water-logged grass, still wet from an early evening shower.

GO HOME....

"Hel-*lo?*" she called anxiously. "All right, who's there?"

Was it all in her mind? Had Francine, before disappearing, gone on an ill-fated midnight stroll?

Something moved in the shadows. The figure hesitated, then stepped out of the shelter of the trees. Hayley stared into the darkness, her eyes struggling to focus. "Who — Simon? Is that you?"

The man snapped on a flashlight and grinned from behind its beam. "Hi, old thing," Simon greeted her. He stood on the soggy lawn dressed in a stylish white turtleneck, cobalt blue windbreaker, and water-resistant jogging pants.

The moment of tension passed.

"Whew!" Hayley exclaimed, giving a nervous laugh. "You scared me half to death! Look at me...I can't stop shaking!" She held her trembling hands before her. "I must look as though I'd seen a ghost!"

"Not a bit of it. You look smashing, as always." Simon took

her hands in his and squeezed them gently. "And I'm not just saying that because of the romantic moonlight, because we have none!" He grinned. Though Simon's manners were not as polished as his brother's, he was just as complimentary.

Hayley gave him a look of gratitude. "That's very kind of you. But what on earth are you doing out here? Have you been following me?" she asked suspiciously.

"No, I'd just come down from the house to find you. I didn't use the torch at first — didn't want to scare you," he explained. "Actually, I wasn't even going to interrupt your reverie, or whatever you call your little stroll. Cook said she saw you come out around half eight, and I was worried. I wanted to make sure you were quite safe."

Hayley's eyes narrowed. "Are you *very* sure you haven't been spying on me this week?"

Simon made a big show of being insulted. "What? I assure you I have better things to do with my time than sneak around." If it were Evan standing there, Hayley might have expected him to continue, smoothly, "Although I might make an exception if *you* were the one being watched." However, Simon refrained from making any such comment. He continued to look wounded. "You must think me quite the Nosey Parker."

Hayley nearly laughed out loud at the expression, which struck her like a missile out of a first-grade name-calling war. "I'm terribly sorry. You're right. What a horrible thing to accuse you of! It's just that…it's the oddest thing! All week I've had the feeling that someone was following me. Isn't that strange?"

Simon looked grim. "I don't know if 'strange' is the word. Have you…actually seen anyone?"

"No. It's more like…oh, you know, when you're sitting in your car, and you get the funny feeling that someone is looking at you, so you look around, and sure enough — the guy in the next car is staring right in your window." Simon nodded. "You see!" Hayley insisted. "Somehow, you just *know. That's* the feeling I've been having all week."

"Oh, I don't doubt you," Simon assured her. "I was just hoping maybe you'd caught a glimpse of the cad. Then perhaps we could do something about it."

"What…do you mean?" Hayley asked, uncomfortably.

"I don't suppose it's any surprise to you. Evan mentioned that he'd warned you about that gardener fellow. We've had our eye on him for quite some time. Since before Francine disappeared, even."

"Carson?" Hayley said dumbly. A chill crept down her spine. *"I had something left for you in your room.…"*

"You look a bit smock-faced." Unexpectedly, Simon leaned forward and touched her cheek.

"Thanks a lot." Hayley kept her voice light but stepped away from his reach.

Simon dropped his arm. "It was an observation," he said simply. "Not a criticism. Are you quite all right?"

"Yes, I'm fine." Hayley waved a hand in the air, dismissing his concern. Feeling a bit shaky, she walked over and leaned against the abandoned pedestal. Within a moment, Simon was at her side. Before she knew what he intended, he had dropped the flashlight, placed both hands upon her waist, and lifted her onto the stone.

He stepped back and surveyed her. *"In a garden shady this holy lady / With reverent cadence and subtle psalm, / Like a black swan as death came on / Poured forth her song in perfect calm...."*

"That's nice." Hayley smiled.

"Auden's *Anthem for St. Cecilia's Day*. It's about Aphrodite, or Venus." Simon leaned casually against the rock beside her. "She used to be there, you know. Right where you're sitting."

Hayley looked down. "I don't follow."

"The statue that was here. It was of Venus — the goddess of love and beauty. A beautiful, life-sized marble figure," Simon said dreamily. "I can barely remember seeing it as a child. It disappeared when I was three."

"Whatever happened to it?"

"Who knows? That *is* the secret of Newhaven," he whispered mysteriously. "One night it was there, the next it was gone. Oh, you should have heard Aunt Theadora and Uncle David when they learned of it! They were furious! Of course, Reverend Archer was thrilled. He always thought the thing was sinful. He took very seriously the fact that it was an image of a pagan god." He laughed. "None of the family ever worshipped it...at least that I know of. But still, he was glad to see it go. The odd thing was, no one ever found the piece. Theadora has connections in the art community. They put out feelers to see if it was being offered on the black market, but there wasn't even a hint of it. Later, it was rumored that the thief was killed before he had the chance to sell it, but the statue never did turn up."

"How romantic...and frightening, all at the same time." Hayley let her thoughts wander, trying to imagine how the statue might have come to disappear.

"You really *do* look like her," Simon said simply. "Venus, I mean."

A feeling of alarm touched Hayley's heart. "Simon...don't."

"I'm serious," he pressed. "What do you expect me to say, Hayley? I know I made a deal with Isabelle, but I'm beginning to care about *you.*" He stepped closer, but Hayley wriggled away from his reach. "*Do* say you feel the same way...."

"Stop it, Simon!" She stared at him in dismay as she slid across the stone. "I *don't* feel the same. Please, don't say another word. This isn't right —" Her heart pounded out a staccato beat.

"But it is!" he insisted, following close behind her. "Don't you see? We're meant to be together, Hayley. You can trust me. Whatever is part of your life should be part of mine, and whatever I have should belong to you."

"Simon, no!" Hayley was thoroughly appalled. How could this be happening again? Two brothers, within one week? "How can you say that? I can't *trust* you. I don't even know you! Besides, if you're willing to cheat on your fiancée now, why should I believe you'd ever stay true to me?"

"It's not the same thing," he protested, taking her hands in his. "I never told Isabelle that I loved her."

"Oh, please!" Hayley sputtered. "Not once?"

"Not —" Simon broke off and met her look of challenge. "All right, maybe I did. But she knew all along it was a business arrangement. Those were just words —"

"Like the ones you're using on me now," Hayley finished for him. "And *this*, Simon," she said firmly, hopping down off the pedestal, "is *action*. I'm going back. Or *you* need to go back." Her eyes softened at his look of dismay. "Please, Simon," she begged him to understand. "I like you. Surely you know that. But I can't be a part of what you're suggesting — and I can't afford to make another enemy here. Be my friend? Don't push. Just let it be."

Simon ran his fingers through his thick chestnut hair and sighed in frustration. "I'll do it. Because I want you to know that *you can trust me.*" He looked at her earnestly. "Promise me that if you have any trouble, any problems at all...*if you need anything,* you will come to me." She hesitated. "*Promise* me that I'm the one you'll come to," he insisted.

"Oh, all right." Hayley would have agreed to almost anything if it meant closing the subject. "But you need to know, we're just friends," she warned him. "This is not a test, Simon, to see if you're worthy. You need to stay true to Isabelle. *Believe me,* I know she's difficult. But you need to stand by her. If you break up with her before you get married, that's your business. But it can't have anything to do with me. Don't you see?"

He nodded sorrowfully. "Yes, I see. But it doesn't change the way I feel about you Hayley. You're a lovely girl." He leaned forward and kissed her gently on the cheek. "Shall I see you back?"

"No, thanks," Hayley declined. The last thing she needed was for anyone to see her walking back into the house with Simon after dark. "You go on ahead. I'll catch up."

Simon glanced around the garden, looking worried. "Are you sure you'll be quite all right?"

"I'm sure," Hayley repeated firmly. "Now, go on. If it'll make you feel better you can leave the light."

Simon did as she suggested, retrieving the flashlight from where he had dropped it and placing it in her hands. With a final, wan smile, he squeezed her fingers gently, turned, and disappeared into the yews.

Hayley shined the beam after him until she was sure he was well away, then turned for one last glimpse of the garden. She caught her breath and killed the beam. For at the far end of the garden was the unmistakable shadow of a third figure, disappearing into the trees. Without thinking, Hayley moved to follow, fear dwarfed by her anger at whoever had been trailing her. The game of cat and mouse was back on.

Only this time, there was a new cat on the hunt.

Thirteen

Whence and what art thou, execrable shape?
John Milton, *Paradise Lost*

The shadow slipped soundlessly from the center of the garden, drifting like the shade toward the stillness of the graveyard. Hayley crept clumsily after it, feeling — absurdly — like a character in a melodramatic movie-of-the-week. "Things like this just don't happen to normal people," she grumbled to herself while creeping, combat-style, between clumps of ground cover. She made a valiant effort, yet "stealth" was not one of her natural gifts; leaves crackled, toes stubbed against rocks. She forced herself to follow at a distance.

The dreadful moment came, not long into her pursuit, when she momentarily lost sight of her target. Fortunately, Hayley realized, her enemy had no idea that he — or she — was being followed, for after slipping through a scrolled gate identical to that on the manor-side of the garden, the figure slowed and began to step more carelessly. Hayley soon caught up by tracking the sound of footsteps tapping against flagstones.

The figure moved steadily in the direction of a low stone wall. Hayley shuddered involuntarily as the destination became clear. Not only was the figure headed *toward* the graveyard, this person was headed straight *into* it. Neither church nor cemetery drew her by day; under the cover of night, both seemed overwhelmingly sinister. It had been long since Hayley had considered God friend; death had always seemed an enemy. She had no desire to meet either one tonight.

Smooth, gray headstones stretched in two long rows: discolored and crumbling, like decaying teeth. Physically, the graveyard was just as she had left it the previous week. But the mood was completely altered. In the blackness, the surrounding gardens had faded from the backdrop. The churchyard was no longer a side-stage to Newhaven; it was the set of its own great drama. Not a stopping point on a greater tour, but a destination in itself. The final destination for dozens. The immediate destination of one. Her enemy stopped and knelt to inspect the smallest block of stone in the yard. One hand drifted over the inscription. At just that moment, Hayley shifted her weight slightly; the soles of her feet slipped against a patch of wet leaves, making a faint squeaking sound.

Hayley held her breath. The figure paused and a head rose in surprise. For a moment, it seemed to consider its next course of action. Then, "You might as well show yourself, Hayley." The voice was familiar, yet strangely strained. "I assume that's you."

As she registered the command, Hayley froze, her feet like lead. She wasn't surprised — or even especially frightened — at being found out. But she could not bring herself to face the confrontation that must follow. Nothing she could imagine would induce her to step forward into that next moment, the one that would forever change her understanding of Newhaven. It wasn't fear for her life that shook her to the core of her being; it was confirmation of the horrible truth she had suspected all week, but had tried to deny.

The figure remained in shadow, but Hayley swayed as recognition took hold.

"Carson." The figure did not move or speak. But Hayley did not need his assent to know her identification was accurate. "You've been following me."

The man stirred, then stood. "There seems to be a lot of that going around," he ground out, his voice taut and low. In the darkness, Hayley felt, more than saw, the intensity of his presence.

Hayley was shaking now, anger mingling with fear. "For crying out loud, hasn't this gone on long enough?" To her dismay, her voice shook as well. She cleared her throat and forced herself to speak more bravely than she felt. "What, exactly, is it that you want from me?" she cried. "Can't you just leave me *alone?*"

"Alone?" Carson spoke dully, as if the word had no meaning for him. "I thought I had been. That's what you asked, isn't it? I haven't talked to you in a week." He made no attempt to step toward her.

Adrenaline finally spurring her to action, Hayley slipped from her position at the cemetery wall and advanced upon her adversary, careful to keep herself at a distance of several arm's lengths. "This isn't about you *talking* to me. This is about you *following* me. Everywhere I go, everything I do…I can feel your nasty little eyes staring at me! Not to mention that horrible note of yours —" she lashed out into the darkness, emotion overcoming reason. "What are you, some kind of sicko? I don't know what you did to poor Francine, but I can assure you I will *not* be your next target." Hayley began to back away, realizing at last the jeopardy she was in. "Stay away from me. I'm warning you."

"Wha —" Carson's outline seemed to shiver. "Staring at you? What are you talking about? What note?" He sounded genuinely incredulous. "What's this about Francine? You can't possibly imagine that I —"

"I mean it!" Hayley backed away, her voice shrill in contrast to his subdued tone. "Don't come any closer! It's a little late to be acting innocent, don't you think? You've as much as admitted you're the one harassing me. I just want to know why." A hint of desperation crept into her tone. "*Why*, Carson? I thought you were such a nice guy! I thought you were my friend —"

"Hayley —" Ignoring her warnings, Carson took several giant steps toward her. And though she knew she should run, Hayley could do nothing but remain rooted in place, watching his hazy outline take on the details of his familiar features. Reaching forward, he grasped her firmly by the arms and gazed into the dark pools that were her eyes. "What on earth can you be thinking? What's gotten into that head of yours? Can you actually think I did something to harm Francine? That I would do something to harm *you*? Do you really think I'm such a monster?" As he spoke, his face contorted like that of a man in torture.

Hayley stared back at the profile that had for days haunted her mind. Though he gripped her arms firmly, there was nothing hurtful in Carson's touch. Though his voice held barely-masked anger, his words held no hint of menace. But it was his eyes: sharp, intense, yet deeply wounded, that most deeply touched her heart.

Standing before him, Hayley found herself incapable of believing her worst fears. This...this was the man whose love for his brother had driven him to adopt the role of parent when he was little more than a boy himself. This was the man who had, for years, tenderly cultivated the beautiful gardens she now cared for with her own hands. This was the man who had befriended her without hesitation when she had been fearful and alone.

This was the man her heart had been telling her — in spite of suspicious circumstances — to trust.

Suddenly, Hayley felt incredibly ashamed.

"No." Her shoulders slumped beneath his heavy hands. "Of course, you're not a monster. I — I'm sorry, Carson." She was unable to raise her eyes above his knees, unable to face his look of disappointment. "That was a stupid thing to say, to even *think* —" Her head ached with unanswered questions. *"I had something left for you in your room..."* What else could he have meant, if not to scare her? The question went unanswered as Carson placed a gentle finger under Hayley's chin and raised her face toward his. There was nothing frightening about him now. His eyes were tender, and he looked as if he might at any moment enfold her in his arms.

"Hayley." She shivered as he spoke her name. "I thought you understood."

"Understood — what?" She was having trouble focusing and found herself wishing he would speak her name again.

Carson laughed. "I would never hurt you, Hayley. I'm — I'm quite...*fond* of you." He sobered. "But then, I thought the flowers made that clear."

"Flowers?" Hayley blinked, thinking back on the countless

beds she had tended that week. "Which flowers do you —" It struck her all at once.

"I had something left for you in your room…"

"I don't know what triggered that sentiment, Mr. Elliott, but…I wish you had not expressed it."

Carson avoiding her the entire week.

The bouquet of honeysuckle and rosemary she'd attributed — unbelievably, foolishly — to Theodora had been Carson's attempt to reach out to her. And she had essentially thrown them back in his face.

"Oh, Carson!" Laughing with nervous energy and relief, she threw herself into his arms. After a momentary pause, he relaxed and began to pat her back awkwardly. By this time, Hayley was shaking with half-laughter, half-sobs. Between gasps, she managed to get out the bulk of her story. Carson listened patiently, silently, until she related the part about the note on her pillow.

"*What* did it say?" The anger was back.

"Uh, 'Go home. Leave what's not yours. I know what you're up to'…or something silly like that. My heavens, what could anyone think I'm 'up to' out here in the gardens? Tampering with the fertilizer?" Hayley tried to joke, hoping to prolong the lighter mood that had begun moments before. "Oh, Carson! I *am* sorry! You must have thought me so rude! I wasn't upset about the flowers. I thought you'd left me that *note*. That's why I came unglued tonight. After being followed —"

Carson stiffened. "You've been followed? Who's been following you?"

Hayley sighed and pulled herself back from his chest, pounding on it gently with one small fist. "Haven't you been *listening?* I don't know! That's why I imagined it must be you." She eyed him curiously. "Which reminds me…what were you doing, there in the shadows tonight? You were following me! Admit it!"

Carson stroked her arm absently, as if his attention were miles away. "You flatter yourself, dear." The comment was disparaging, but he softened it with a wink. "Actually, I'd been out for a walk. I haven't been sleeping well lately. See over there?" He pointed to a glow beyond the churchyard. "Just the other side of the wall? That's the cottage I share with Gabe. I often step over to the gardens late at night — when it's cool, and I can be alone. It's hard to enjoy them during the day, with Theadora grousing about. Tonight I just happened by when I saw the torch light…." Carson let his hands fall from her arms and drew back slightly. His movement was almost imperceptible, but Hayley felt it to the core of her soul. "I wasn't trying to sneak about. It just seemed like you wanted to be alone."

Hayley felt her cheeks flush hotly. *He's jealous.…* "Carson —" She reached out to touch his sleeve.

"I know, I know. It's none of my business whom you like. True enough. But…I consider us friends, Hayley. I feel…protective of you. I want you to be careful." Hayley tried to read his face. But by pulling away, Carson had effectively masked his expression in darkness. "You needn't feel defensive. This isn't personal." His voice was carefully devoid of emotion. "I'd warn any woman getting involved with a Harrington. And if you just let me explain, I think you'll see why."

Clasping his calloused hands around Hayley's own, Carson drew her toward the low wall, seated himself upon the stones, and indicated that she should do likewise. Moving close,

Hayley found herself searching his face once more. But the man remained unreadable.

"I told you once that I've had a hard time adjusting to being a parent. I rather let you think I'd had trouble with Gabe, but that's not true — and hardly fair to him. He's a decent lad. Never given me a bit of trouble. No." Carson sighed and paused so long, Hayley began to wonder if he might not continue. Finally, he took a deep breath and went on. "The trouble came with Jennifer. Our sister."

Hayley drew a deep breath as Gabriel's words echoed in her head. When she'd asked why Carson hadn't pursued Francine, the boy had seemed to make reference to a sister.

"She was always a wild one, our Jenny!" Carson laughed. "She and Gabe are fairly close in age, but I tell you — she was ages ahead of him in terms of getting into mischief. It wasn't so bad when we were younger. I was the protective older brother who constantly pulled her out of scrapes. She adored me, and I doted on her — despite the fact that she could be aggravating at times. We got along famously, really.

"But then Mother died. Jenny was eleven at the time. I don't think she knew what to do with her emotions, how to process them. She went a little nuts after that. She was a difficult pre-teen; a terror when she got older. I anticipated there'd be problems when she started dating the high school boys. But she never did." Carson's voice was grim. "She had her sights set on older men." He sighed. "I suppose, all things being what they are, it was only a matter of time before it happened."

The muscles in Hayley's stomach tightened. It was impossible not to concede the obvious. "Evan."

"As you say," Carson agreed dryly. "Evan."

Hayley reflected on the feelings of discomfort the older

Harrington had stirred within her. He was smooth, to be sure. Too smooth. If she hadn't been so frightened, if she'd had more confidence in her ability to handle men, would she have been ensnared by him, just as Jenny had? It was largely due to Carson's disapproval that Hayley had managed to extricate herself from the beginnings of that relationship. A wave of gratitude swept over her, and she was glad that Carson felt comfortable confiding in her.

"How old is Jenny?" she questioned, urging him to continue.

"She was barely seventeen at the time." Carson spoke through clenched teeth. "Eighteen now."

Hayley mulled this over. "Obviously they're not together anymore. How did you manage to break them apart?"

"I had nothing to do with it." Carson sounded ready to explode. "Although I would have done anything in my power to get her away from him while there was still time. I even tried to get Theadora to help me, but she refused."

"She actually took Evan's side?" Hayley was surprised. She'd been under the impression little love was lost between the two.

"It's not so much that she helped him. She simply wouldn't get involved. Said she wasn't about to tell her family their business. Ha!" He laughed, but there was no humor to the sound. "That would be a first."

Hayley let the last comment pass. "So what happened with your sister?" she prodded.

Carson swallowed hard. "The worst thing that *could* happen. Jenny got pregnant."

"No —" Instinctively, Hayley took his hand to comfort him, but Carson's fingers remained stiff and unresponsive against hers.

"She didn't even tell me." He pulled his hand from Hayley's and ran his fingers distractedly through his unruly hair. "She didn't feel she could come to me. Her brother! I was the only parent she had," he moaned. "And I failed her."

"Carson," Hayley tried sympathetically, "that's not what that means. It's hard for any girl to —"

Carson kept right on talking. "I knew something was wrong. She started getting depressed. It just kept getting worse and worse. Then, one day out of the blue, she and Evan just stopped seeing each other. I couldn't believe it! Of course, I was thrilled. Jenny didn't want to talk to me about it — I wonder why?" he asked bitterly. "I figured it was just normal grieving, that she'd get over him on her own. Finally, after several months, she disappeared. No note. Nothing."

There was silence for a moment as Hayley let this sink in. "How did you find out she was pregnant?"

"I had a little — talk with Evan," Carson hedged. "He slipped up, figuring that I already knew. I tried to get him to tell me where she'd gone, but he claimed — still claims — he doesn't know."

"Did she…? Was she still…?" Hayley couldn't bring herself to finish the question.

"I don't know, Hayley." Carson rested his head in his hands wearily. "I can't imagine that she would have gotten an abortion. But then, I'm not in her shoes. I don't know what she was feeling, to what she might have felt driven. All I can do is wait — and hope — and pray that she'll come home."

"It must be awkward," Hayley said realizing the magnitude of her understatement even as she spoke, "working here after all that's happened."

"I loathe the Harringtons," Carson admitted. "And I'd sacrifice anything to be able to leave — except Jenny. I can't risk the chance that she might come back and not find her family here. That's why Gabe and I have stayed. But someday…" His voice trailed away as his thoughts returned to the events that had caused the destruction of his family.

Hayley tried to think of some way to cheer him. "You know, I owe you one, for steering me away from Evan," she said, playfully smoothing a crease in the fabric of his sleeve.

"Evan!" Carson snorted, hatred evident on his face. "I wouldn't wish him on my worst enemy." Hayley drew back, stung. "Of course, my advice probably just made your decision easier," he said coldly.

"My…decision?"

"Which rich brother to give your heart to," Carson bit out. "I guess you made your choice. You and Simon were looking pretty cozy when I arrived on the scene."

"Carson, I —"

The man rose abruptly. "It doesn't matter, Hayley. Do as you please." He turned and began his retreat toward the cottage, looking defeated.

Hayley moved as if to follow. How could he say such a thing? Had she been mistaken? Didn't he care for her? "Carson, please! I —" She stopped in her tracks as his words sank in. *It doesn't matter, Hayley.*

Of course it didn't.

"I wouldn't wish him on my worst enemy."

"I'd warn any woman getting involved with a Harrington."

Gabriel, laughing. *"On top of everything else, he's smitten."*

"Can you actually think I did something to harm Francine?"

Her heart sank at the thought, even as she realized it was true: Carson's behavior toward her stemmed from a misplaced sense of brotherly concern, nothing more.

Flustered, Hayley sat back on the rock wall and let him go without another word.

Left alone amongst the gravestones, she felt an intensification of the loneliness that had long haunted her. How had she so completely misinterpreted Carson's feelings for her? Had the events of the week completely addled her brain? Surely, Evan — ever the playboy — had made a fair attempt at courting her. Simon — oh, what was she to think of Simon? Was he sincere in admitting that he had feelings for her? Or was he simply experiencing pre-wedding jitters? *Who wouldn't, if he were marrying Isabelle?* Hayley pushed the unkind thought aside. But Carson was not flirting. Carson was simply befriending. She should be — she *was* — grateful for that.

No doubt her confusion stemmed from experiencing a week in which her life was totally out of control — a state she had avoided as much as possible since her parents' deaths. No, Carson was nothing more than a friend, like Gabe. Hayley resolved to push all feelings of disappointment aside. At least the two of them were talking again. The misunderstanding regarding the flowers was now cleared up. Carson had tried to make her feel welcome, and poor communication had botched the effort. But now all was well. Everything was finally out in the open.

Hayley sighed and stood, pointing herself back in the direction of the manor, then — her memory kicking in — she paused on impulse and knelt at the gravestone which had briefly captured Carson's attention.

Time stood still; her heart skipped a beat as the inscription swam before her unbelieving eyes:

JONATHAN BUCKMAN

1949-1969

Fourteen

There are secrets in all families.
George Farquhar, *The Beaux Stratagem*

Hayley's hands flew like the hands of a crazed barber, wildly scattering twigs and leaves as she carved at the overgrown shrub before her. The branches were thick and healthy, her clippers slightly dull, but Hayley was not slowed by the physical challenge. Absentmindedly, but enthusiastically, she worked — snipping, slicing, shearing all new growth in her path — while her thoughts turned again and again to the previous night's shocking discovery.

She'd been up half the night playing out one explanation after another; the sleep she *had* gotten was fitful at best. At first, she had tried to dismiss the situation as a coincidence. "Buckman" was a customary English name, was it not? "Jonathan" more common yet? Even more comforting was the fact that Hayley's father had died in 1993, not 1969. Hayley herself had not been born until 1971. There was no theory that could explain her existence apart from her father's. Jon Buckman — *her* Jon Buckman — had lost his life at the young age of forty-four; the man in Newhaven's cemetery had died even more tragically at twenty.

Yet questions continued to gnaw at her mind. Was the man another relative, perhaps? That was ridiculous. No normal family could generate *two* Jon Buckmans born in 1949 — that *was* the year of her father's birth, she was sure. No matter how hard she tried to explain away the name on the gravestone, Hayley's explanations fell flat. It was all too bizarre to be mere coincidence.

But what did it mean? And how could this have come about? No one had reason to set a trap for her. Even if they did, Hayley herself was the one responsible for her coming to Newhaven. She had learned about the internship while at school and decided on her own to apply. No outside force had engineered her interest or forced the application process.

Or had it?

Hayley tightened her grip on the shears. Beads of sweat trickled down her well-toned arms, and her skin itched beneath her cotton shirt and canvas shorts. Her pace increased as she reflected angrily on recent events.

Things had started out innocently enough. Back in the fall she had discovered, then pursued, the internship because of her fascination with England. The fact that the estate was located in the Chilterns — an area remembered fondly by her father — simply added to the appeal; as if her own interest in the country itself wasn't enough, Hayley was overjoyed by the prospect of visiting the land her parents had once loved. She had hoped that somehow her trip might allow her to feel close to them once again. Yet when the application process had begun, events had moved with a haste that seemed disturbing, even to Hayley.

Her thoughts flashed back to her conversation with Carson on the day of her arrival:

"Theadora always asks for a portfolio.... You were rung up for a telephone interview?"

"Well...no. Is that so terribly unusual?" she had responded, naively.

Still more ominous were Carson's words to Theadora the following day: *"I just want to know what you're really up to. This whole thing stinks, and it's obvious you're the one making the calls."*

Hayley swallowed hard and flailed at a lush, green branch. Clearly, Carson had suspected something from the very beginning, although how — or why — he'd keyed in to Jon Buckman's gravestone was unclear. Yet in at least one matter, Hayley was certain Carson was right on target: in the drama of Newhaven, Theadora was the master puppeteer.

The woman must have been the author of Hayley's warning after all. But why? Why bring Hayley to Newhaven in the first place, if the only goal was to frighten her away? What could Theadora possibly gain by tormenting a young woman who shared a name with a man buried at her estate over two decades before?

There was only one way to find out.

Hayley cast a look of disgust upon the butchered tree beneath her shears and set out for the house with one goal in mind: cutting an even more formidable target down to size.

Newhaven's great halls echoed with the emptiness and lack of warmth for which it was, to Hayley, now known. Despite her anger and confusion, the young woman felt her fury diminish slightly as she stomped down the stark corridor. No matter what the situation, it was difficult to feel intimidating in such overwhelming surroundings.

She tried to gather her emotional fortitude. *I'm not a toy. No one has the right to play with me like this. I'll just come right out and demand that Theadora tell me what's going on. What's the worst that can happen?* Thoughts of Francine came to mind, but Hayley hastily dismissed them. *Nothing but speculation there. She probably just had a tiff with Carson.* The thought disturbed Hayley and actually distracted her for a moment. She paused before ascending the sweeping staircase.

That would mean Francine might come back. At any time. Hayley's uneasiness increased as she started to climb. *What then?* There was nothing so indispensable as an intern vying for the same position desired by the girlfriend of the head gardener.

Hayley reached the second floor and turned her focus back to her plan of attack. She'd considered following protocol, asking Ellen to announce her arrival to Theadora, but had decided instead to use the element of surprise; whatever Theadora chose to verbally admit would be confirmed or denied by her eyes.

That left Hayley with the unappealing prospect of conducting a room-by-room search that might eventually lead to Theadora, but might also bring her face to face with Simon, Isabelle, or Evan. Hayley moaned, a sour feeling stirring in the pit of her stomach. *Oh, well. I always say I like a challenge. Here's my chance to prove it.*

She rested at the top of the staircase, weighing her choices. To the left lay her guest room, a guest bath and — if she remembered correctly from Ellen's brisk tour — a dozen other guest rooms that had for years remained vacant. To the right, Hayley hazily recalled, was the wing that housed the family's living quarters. She had no idea how Theadora spent her days when not in the gardens, but it seemed as good a place as any to begin her search.

Timber-paneled walls stretched out before her, their dark tone reflecting the color of Hayley's mood. Stepping resolutely toward the door on her right, she took a deep breath and reached for a well-worn brass knob. The hardware rattled and turned under her fingers, but although Hayley pressed her weight against the wood, the door remained firmly in place.

"It figures," she grunted and backed up to survey her dilemma. Dark eyes squinted and scanned the cavernous hall. One after another, each frame was blocked by a solid-looking door. Probably they all were locked.

Hayley tested her theory, moving down the corridor, testing one doorknob after the next; her suspicion was quickly confirmed.

"Great. Now what?" Wounded pride gave way to irritation as she considered how to cross the unexpected hurdle in her path. For a moment, she imagined herself employing an elaborate plan to spirit the master keys away from Ellen. She shook her head at the absurdity of the thought. "Yeah, right. I think I saw a few too many *I Love Lucy* episodes in my childhood." Briefly, she considered going to Carson or Gabe, but realized that they had a lesser chance than she of gaining access to the main house.

Hayley was still weighing her options when a door at the end of the hall opened a crack.

"The subject is *closed.*" Theadora's raised voice identified her as clearly as did her words. "I've had enough of your opinions. In fact, I've had enough of *you*. You are *excused*."

"But —" a sullen voice protested from the doorway.

"Not another word!" The finality in her tone allowed no room for argument.

The door opened wide, and a dismal-looking figure stepped into the hallway. His fists clenched at his side, jaw set in anger, Evan Harrington looked like nothing so much as a rebellious school boy being sentenced to bed without supper.

The man's eyes fell upon Hayley and his jaw slackened. Glancing back over his shoulder, he appeared for a moment to be reconsidering his retreat. Then, apparently thinking better of it, he gave Hayley a cool nod, straightened his broad shoulders, and swept past her with a look of dignity seemingly meant to decry his momentary lapse in composure.

Hayley let him go without objection. *As if I care how you act toward me*, she scoffed. Her eyes drifted to the doorway ahead. *I've got way bigger fish to fry than you, buster.* She stepped forward with purpose and resolve, prepared to do mental battle with the woman who had, moments earlier, effectively chewed up and spit out one of the most dynamic and self-possessed men Hayley had ever met.

At the door, she nearly paused, but forced herself to push onward.

She stepped into the room, taking a moment to gain her bearings. That it was a study was immediately clear. Massive bookshelves lined the high-beamed walls, and a scarlet armchair beckoned invitingly from the large bay window by which it was carefully positioned to capitalize on the early morning light. Beneath Hayley's feet lay a thick Oriental carpet woven of rich green and gold; to her right, a small, elegant, white marble fireplace stood empty and cold. But it was the oversized maple desk, or rather its occupant, that caught and held Hayley's gaze.

Hayley was not a nosy person, yet in recent days she'd had no choice but to observe the varied moods of her enigmatic employer. At Theadora's weakest moments, she had impressed Hayley as being an eminently domineering, incredibly isolated older woman. At her strongest, she had appeared no less powerful than the most charismatic world leader. But as Hayley now approached, Theadora sat staring at her hands, a blank expression on her face: the very picture of a woman who had been broken — by disappointment? Discouragement? Perhaps even by loneliness?

Hayley mentally flicked the thought away like a pesky fly. *If Theadora's lonely, it's because she brought it upon herself. You can only treat people so poorly before they begin to stand up for themselves.* The reasoning did not hold up where Evan was concerned; Hayley could not imagine the man fighting for some noble cause. But when applied to her own situation, it gave her the tiny boost of confidence she needed in order to proceed.

"Theadora." Hayley concentrated on keeping her voice even.

Red rims traced circles around eyes dulled by age. The tan twill jacket that protected her from the manor chill hung heavily on her shoulders. Theadora shifted her gaze but appeared to look right through Hayley.

The young woman licked red, bitten lips nervously. "Theadora," she tried again, more forcefully this time. "I need to talk to you. I believe you have some explaining to do." When the woman failed to rally before her, Hayley felt a twinge of alarm and relented. "If this is a bad time, I can come back. But...," she faltered, "I really *do* think we have something critical to discuss."

Theadora's eyes narrowed as she tried to focus on Hayley's words. "Explaining?" she mused, her stare glassy. "Mm, yes. I suppose that's true. Well, come in then. Don't just stand there. Have a seat." The words were pure Theadora, but her behavior remained uncharacteristically meek.

Hayley did as she was instructed, drawing a golden-toned Windsor chair up to the edge of Theadora's desk. She immediately regretted her action; Theadora was now unmistakably in the position of power. It would have been wiser to move to one of the armchairs positioned near the fireplace. But as she watched the older woman's gaze drift aimlessly about the room, Hayley realized that at that moment, she had little to fear from the woman she had begun to consider her enemy.

Despite her anger, Hayley could not help but ask, "Are you all right, Theadora? You...really don't seem yourself."

Theadora looked back at her in surprise, as if astonished by Hayley's perception. "I — I'm afraid I'm feeling quite tired this afternoon."

"Would you like me to leave?" Hayley offered reluctantly. "I could come back later."

"That won't be necessary." Apparently motivated by Hayley's recognition of her weakness, Theadora seemed to attempt to compose herself. "You say I have some explaining to do?" She was calm, exhibiting no hint of concern.

Relieved to no longer find herself worrying about Theadora's state of mind, Hayley turned gratefully to the matter at hand. "That's right." Her clear brown eyes sought out

Theadora's watery ones. Their gaze met and held. Convinced that Theadora was now fully present, Hayley decided to waste no further time. "Theadora, who was Jonathan Buckman?"

Theadora's upper lip twitched. Her black eyes flashed, and her face was momentarily graced by an expression Hayley could not identify. Seconds later, the mask was back in place. "I should have thought you knew. Of course, Jonathan was your father, Hayley."

Hayley took a deep breath, trying unsuccessfully to keep the room from swirling. She plunged onward. "No, I mean *your* Jonathan Buckman. The one buried in the graveyard."

Theadora gave her a look of disdain. "*My* Jon Buckman, as you call him, was your Jon Buckman. Or rather, I should say, your *mother's* Jon Buckman."

This can't be happening. It can't be true.... "But that's not poss —" Dozens of unanswered questions darted across Hayley's mind; she found herself unable to offer up a single one.

"I wondered if you'd find the gravestone. It didn't seem likely, but one never knows," Theadora mused. She turned back to Hayley and peered at her curiously, real interest returning to her small black eyes. "Do you mean to tell me you really hadn't any idea?"

Hayley fought back her fury. "Any idea? Are you *kidding?*" All the eloquent arguments she had prepared vanished from her mind. "What are you *talking* about? How could you summon me here and not *tell* me who you are — who I am?" To her dismay, she sounded more like an injured child than a rightfully angered professional.

"I thought perhaps you already knew," Theadora offered, as

if that were explanation enough. Caught by Hayley's piercing stare, she continued, "After all, *you* were the one who applied to come to Newhaven. I might ask the same thing of you. How could you not inform me that you were my grandchild? Did you think I wouldn't recognize the name?" She snorted derisively, a hint of the old Theadora returning. "My confidential secretary pulled your application from the file and brought it to my immediate attention. Of course I followed through."

"What are you saying?" Hayley dug dirt-encrusted nails into the arm of her chair. "That I came here with some ulterior motive?" The thought was too absurd to be believed. She was completely unprepared for the turn the conversation was taking.

"I'm sure I don't know," Theadora replied acidly. "Why else would you come?"

"Because I — I wanted to see England." The explanation sounded lame, even to her ears. "I wanted to serve my internship in the country that once was my parents' home."

"And you had no idea who I was?" It was clear from Theadora's tone that she considered the suggestion preposterous.

"No!" Hayley was on the edge of her chair now. "Absolutely not!" Suddenly, she felt unexpectedly defensive. "If you thought I had some sinister plot in mind, why on earth did you ask me to come?"

"I'm sure I didn't know what you had in mind." Theadora sighed dramatically.

"Besides," Hayley's eyes narrowed, her indignation returning, "*you're* the one who insisted that I come right away. What was that all about? You didn't care a fig about my qualifications.

You expect me to replace a woman who disappeared under mysterious circumstances —"

"Oh, that." Theadora waved a skinny hand in the air, her paper-like skin looking anemic in the warm-toned room. "There wasn't anything mysterious about it at all. I simply excused Francine from her duties."

"And you thought it necessary for her to leave that night?" Hayley sounded unconvinced. "Without saying good-bye to anyone?"

"I did not think it would be wise to allow her to share what she knew with anyone else at Newhaven. As I said, I had no idea what you were about. It seemed wise for me to keep control of the situation as best I could." *Control.* In that split second, Hayley realized that for all Theadora's unpleasant characteristics, the two of them were not dissimilar.

That's because she's my grandmother.

The reality of it hit her all at once. "No, no. This isn't possible," she argued frantically. "Your — *this* Jon Buckman died in 1969. I wasn't born until 1971. You've made a terrible mistake. It's just a coincidence. Besides, my father —"

"It is not a coincidence, my dear." Theadora ignored Hayley's denial, sounding completely sure of herself. "No doubt your mother altered records to keep us from finding you. That would be simple enough, I would suppose, in a country like America. And apparently, she gave you the legal name Buckman, although your parents never married." Ill-concealed contempt crept into her speech. "The truth is clear to me. You confirmed my suspicions when you gave your mother's name on your application. You look so much like Camilla...." Her voice trailed off as the hint of loneliness returned to her expression. "Here —" She interrupted her own thoughts and opened one heavy desk drawer. "I will prove it. I have your mother's picture." Bony hands reached into the depths and pulled forth a small stack of black and white images.

The woman captured on film could have been Hayley's double.

"Mama —" Hayley's voice was a whisper. She touched the photographs with reverent fingers, as if afraid the prints would crumble into fairy dust. A surge of longing welled up within her; she looked across at Theadora and realized that the woman was caught up with emotions, the same as she.

Her voice cracked as anger faded into pain. "But *why?* Why didn't anyone tell me…?" Even in her state of confusion, Hayley recognized that Theadora was less than the ideal grandmother. But her parents' deception about the woman's existence seemed almost too much to grasp.

For once, Theadora was without a sharp reply. The two women sat, face to face, each grappling with her pain. After an extended silence, Hayley realized that once more, the woman across from her was looking unusually pale and subdued. At that moment, Hayley herself wanted nothing more than time to process the input that threatened to send her into overload.

"Theadora, I think we should take some time — let this go for now," she suggested in a small voice. "I'm sure there's…much more to say. But let's just hold this for a moment and talk once we've both had time to collect our thoughts."

Theadora was not of a mind to argue. "I believe that would be best."

Hayley stood and walked stiffly to the door, the photos still clutched in her clammy hand.

"Hayley." Theadora's voice stopped her. The younger woman spun on her heel.

Seated behind her great desk, Theadora looked smaller and more helpless than Hayley would have thought possible. She hesitated a moment, then offered, weakly, "I am truly sorry about your father."

Jon Buckman 1949-1969

"But —" Hayley began, then stopped herself. "Thank you." She turned away and bit back the questions forming on her lips.

For some reason, Theadora was convinced that her father had died in 1969. She had no idea that Jon Buckman had lived another twenty-four years after leaving England. She did not realize that he and Camilla were married...that their daughter was not illegitimate. Hayley herself was the only one who knew.

And she wasn't about to share her knowledge.

It wasn't much of an edge. But if she were to find out what was really going on, Hayley would need every advantage she could get.

Fifteen

❦

Depart, I say, and let us have done with you.
In the name of God, go!
Oliver Cromwell, addressing the Rump Parliment,
April 20, 1653

Hayley stumbled down the hallway; her mind frozen, instincts directed her retreat. Her focus centered simply on reaching the haven of her room where she could shut herself away until she could make some sense of this nightmare. Only a few steps more....

To Hayley's dismay, the door to a nearby room swung open and a stunning blonde in cool sage linen graced the corridor. Hayley fought the urge to curse under her breath. Over the past week, she and Isabelle had crossed paths briefly — and with forced civility — on numerous occasions, but she'd had no idea the woman was sleeping just down the hall. Of all the moments to run into her, this was the worst. Under other circumstances, Hayley might have risen to the challenge. But now, she had neither the energy nor the desire to engage in a battle of wits — *or lack thereof. Not that it matters. Since last week's picnic, she's avoided me like the plague. She's not likely to initiate contact now. If I can just slip inside my room....*

"What is wrong with you?" Hayley's luck suddenly ran out. Violet eyes drifted over the brunette's disheveled clothing and vacant stare, and Isabelle's pouty mouth was transformed by a slow, satisfied smile. "You look positively dreadful."

Hayley bit back a scathing retort. *Don't let her pull you in.* "I'm not feeling well. I just need a little rest —" She fumbled with her doorknob, hoping the other woman would take the hint.

Isabelle was apparently not the perceptive type. "I understand you've had words with Evan." Her pleasure was clearly evident; she made no effort to conceal it. "You know, he's not one to be trifled with. I'd be careful if I were you. One never knows what might happen."

Hayley finally had the door unlocked, but although she could have made her escape, Isabelle's last comment finally pushed her over the edge. The woman clearly seemed pleased with whatever she thought she knew. Hayley couldn't help but think about her interaction with Simon. If Isabelle knew about *that*, she might not feel so smug....

No. Telling her was not an option. Despite her anger, Hayley could never intentionally cause another human being pain. Still...if she were ever to have any peace, Isabelle would have to be put in her place. Keeping one hand on the doorknob, Hayley threw her dark hair over her shoulder and fixed the woman with an icy glare.

"Oh, and is that supposed to frighten me?" She measured out each word with care. "And I suppose you all expected me to run away when Evan warned me about Francine's 'mysterious' disappearance?" Her expression turned to one of disgust. "Nice try, but I happen to know there wasn't anything mysterious about it. I have no idea what your game is, but you might as well know, you don't scare me a bit. Not one of you. As far as I'm concerned, you can keep your little glares, your snippy little comments, your mean-spirited threat —"

"Oh, those weren't threats," Isabelle said mildly. "They were simply warnings. For your own good."

"My own good? Ha!" To her dismay, Hayley realized she was arguing like a child. She tried to compose herself. "I can take responsibility for my own well being, thank you very much," she said slowly. "If you would just —" As she spoke, Isabelle's words sank in. 'Threats'? Plural? Isabelle wasn't referring to a single attempt at intimidation; she was admitting to multiple offenses. Of course.

The picnic.

The note.

Hayley drew a deep breath. "And just *what*," she leveled her eyes and tone, "did you hope to accomplish by leaving your little hate note on my pillow?"

Isabelle opened her eyes wide and shrugged innocently. "There was nothing hateful about it. I merely suggested that for you to leave would be best."

Hayley felt the urge to reach across and shake her. "Oh, really? And what was that bit about leaving what isn't mine? Do you really think I would set my sights on someone else's fiancé?"

The logic seemed to escape Isabelle's understanding. "Why not?"

Hayley sighed in exasperation. She almost felt sorry for this woman. "*Because*...it's just as you said. He isn't mine." *For crying out loud, when is she going to let go of this?* "I *promise* you,

I've no desire to take something that doesn't belong to me."

Isabelle looked unconvinced. "I'm sure Evan will be thrilled to hear that," she commented dryly.

By this time, Hayley was thoroughly exasperated. "Evan? Now what has he got to do with anything?"

Isabelle at last had no response.

"Look," Hayley began, "I really *don't* know what you're talking about. If there's something that needs to cleared up here, I'd be happy to —"

"There's no need to play innocent," Isabelle broke in. "Everyone knows why you're here."

Hayley gaped at her. "Why I'm…here?"

"What is it they say? The apple doesn't fall far from the tree?" her adversary said cryptically. "You may have thought you'd get away with it, but they've sussed you out. It's obvious you've come back to finish what your father began." Stepping closer to Hayley, she whispered, "Everyone knows. Simon would kill me if he knew I'd told you. But I'd rather see you go now. There will only be more trouble if you stay." Hayley thought she detected a hint of apprehension. But was it the threat of losing her fiancé, or something more sinister that had struck fear in Isabelle's eyes? "No one in the family wants you here," Isabelle warned. "You're too much of a threat. If you stay, you won't get what you've come for. They'll step in before they let you get away with it."

Hayley stared at her, shaken. "Get away with *what?*"

Isabelle continued to ignore her protests. "I really *am* telling you this for your own good," she insisted. Her cat-like eyes widened in earnestness, and she suddenly looked very young. For a moment, Hayley nearly believed her. "If you keep on, they'll just use you to get what they need for themselves. Do you really think that Evan — or Simon—" she scoffed, "would actually care for *you?* The illegitimate gardener?" Hayley winced. The most painful insults are the ones based on truth. "Do us all a favor and go before this all gets any uglier. Believe me —" Her voice conveyed total conviction. "It will get sticky if you stay."

Then, without another word, the storm drifted away, leaving a thoroughly shaken Hayley in her wake.

Sixteen

And he shall be a sanctuary.
Isaiah 8:13

In her mind's eye, her sanctuary was represented by a welcoming glow. Hayley paused among the granite markers, trying to locate the source of light that Carson had, the night before, identified as "the cottage I share with Gabe."

The building was not difficult to find. During Hayley's first visit to the cemetery, she had easily overlooked it, her attention having been focused upon the affable cleric and her own feelings of unrest. Last night, also, the small house had escaped her notice, remaining hidden under the blanket of nightfall. But now, she saw it as clear as day, leaning jauntily on the hillside beyond the chapel. Perhaps it was simply due to the claustrophobic feelings she had felt inside the manor, but to Hayley, the cottage appeared more cheery and welcoming than any dwelling she had ever seen.

She stepped over the low stone wall and advanced upon the tiny building with both trepidation and hope. The trepidation was reasonable, considering she still had a great deal to settle with the head gardener — not the least of which was his role in bringing her to Newhaven and his knowledge about her father. The hope was harder to explain. Yet, somehow — instinctively — Hayley felt that Carson and Gabe's home was, for her, a safe place.

The young woman paused before the ivy-covered entrance, her cheeks flushed scarlet. She felt awkward, running to Carson ("and Gabe," she reminded herself) in her time of need; yet, it seemed to her the one course of action that made sense in her rapidly crumbling world.

She knocked on the massive wooden door and waited expectantly. Moments later, it swung open on its hinges to reveal a round-cheeked Carson, munching enthusiastically on a thick slice of gingerbread. At the sight of her, his eyes widened and his mouth opened slightly, causing several sticky-looking crumbs to fall from his lips.

Hayley could not keep from laughing when she saw the look of dismay on his face.

"Sorry!" he mumbled through his dinner, then swallowed purposefully. A trail of ginger crumbs trickled down the front of his navy henley. "What a pig I must seem! We don't often get visitors. I figured it must be Gabe, up to some nonsense."

"No problem," she assured him brightly. There was a minute of awkward silence as she waited for him to invite her inside. For a moment, it looked like Carson might actually fail to do so. He looked at her curiously, as though expecting her to state the purpose of her visit. When Hayley remained silent, he smiled tentatively and stepped back into the house. Thankfully, he seemed determined to leave behind them their skirmish regarding Simon.

"Please, do come in," he offered graciously. Hayley did so, gratefully.

She had felt cheered by the cottage's outside appearance. The sight within instantly triggered feelings of "home."

The rooms were small. Even the ceilings were low, and as Carson wandered about, he reminded Hayley of a giant Alice who had consumed the cookie labeled "Eat me." *Or was it the bottle marked "Drink me"?*

Either way, Carson seemed too large for his surroundings. But just as he had done in the Mini, he seemed to manage his gangly limbs and move about quite easily within the cramped quarters. Hayley peered about the room, which seemed to be a combination dining area/living space. In one corner stood a precariously-leaning table of robin's egg blue, which held the remnants of Carson's lunch. All around them, dusty books, faded pictures, and assorted family mementos overflowed from brightly-painted cabinets and wonderfully distressed cupboards. In contrast to the garish opulence of the manor, the cottage seemed comfortable and familiar, like an old friend.

Normally, Hayley loathed spending sunny afternoons indoors. But after her morning, spent working in the warm sun, and the excitement of her recent confrontations with Theadora and Isabelle, the cool of the cottage was tremendously soothing. Hayley tucked herself into a lumpy, orange-and-yellow armchair situated by the fireplace and smiled timidly at her host, who still appeared bewildered by her presence.

"Would you like some dinner?" Carson tried, eyeing her curiously. "I've just had some grilled kidneys. I'd be happy to broil some more if you'd like."

Hayley shuddered at the prospect. The mere thought of food — and in particular any sort of kidney — caused a wave of nausea to strike. "No, thank you. Really, I shouldn't have interrupted your meal. But I wanted to talk to you, and I thought this might be the best time to find you at home."

"That's quite all right." Carson assured her. "I've finished now. Are you sure you won't have something to drink? Tea, perhaps? No? All right then." He settled onto the worn chesterfield sofa beside her chair. "You have my full attention. What's on your mind?"

Hayley thought for a moment, weighing how to begin. One didn't just barge into someone's house, announce that she had been employed under false pretenses, and accuse her host of being involved. Her gracefully-shaped eyebrows furrowed together as she tried to think of a smooth opening.

Darkly tanned fingers reached across and patted her hand. "Are you quite all right?" Concern touched both Carson's voice and his eyes. His grip tightened. "Have you been followed again?"

"Oh, it's not that." His remark actually caught Hayley off guard. She'd dealt with so many unexpected issues in the past half day, she'd had no time to think about a potential stalker. "No, it's just that —" She swallowed hard. "Carson, I want to talk to you about something, and I need for you not to get angry with me for asking."

Something flickered in his deep green eyes, but he gave no hint of alarm. "Fire away."

"Okay." Hayley took a deep breath and let the bomb fall. "Apparently, Theadora Harrington is my...grandmother." She tried to assess Carson's reaction, but for once, his eyes gave away nothing. She continued nervously, "My parents emigrated to America before I was born. They *never* told me that I had any relatives left in England. As a matter of fact, they rarely spoke of their homeland at all." She tugged at a stray thread poking out from the chair's arm.

"Once, in college, I tried to plan a trip to England, but my folks talked me out of it. Also, they were completely against my becoming a gardener. As far as I can tell, they had no intention of ever allowing me to come to England, or learning about their — our — family. My mother taught me about working the earth. But my father never was comfortable with my love for gardening. I guess it reminded him too much of what they'd left behind." Again, she looked to him for a reaction, but Carson's face remained a mask of non-emotion.

"I applied for this internship," she pushed on, "because I wanted to visit England and I knew my parents were from this general area. They died several years ago, and I wanted to establish some sort of connection. But I had no idea what I was walking into." The words rushed out in a torrent now. "Theadora has admitted that she knew who I was before she even sent for me. What I need to know is...did you know, too?" Hayley bit her lip and waited for his response.

During her hurried speech, Carson had watched her closely. Now, his eyes drifted to the sunny, white-painted windowsill. He responded slowly, "So you are a Harrington, then." There was bitterness to his tone. "I suspected as much." He met her accusing eyes. "But I didn't know for sure."

"How did you know?"

"It was the little things. The way you were hired. Your surname. The way those two bloody fools were behaving. That makes you second or third cousins, then, doesn't it? Not to worry," he said dryly. His old rudeness had returned. "It's a rather remote connection I'd say. I wouldn't let that stop you."

Hayley's irritation grew, but she was determined not to let another misunderstanding come between them. "Stop me from what? Are you still back on the whole Simon thing? Really, Carson," she chastised him. "Get over it, already! I realize you don't like the guy, but you don't have to let your grudge affect everything else. You're just looking for something to be mad about," she accused. Carson simply glowered at her.

Hayley regretted the words as soon as they were out of her mouth. After all, this was a man whose family was nearly destroyed by the Harringtons and whose girlfriend had mysteriously been spirited away by their hands. "Look," she tried again. "I *am* sorry about Jenny." Her voice was gentle. "And about Francine."

Carson blinked at her. "Francine? What has she to do with all this?"

"Well…," Hayley hesitated. "The good news is, nothing at all sinister happened to her. The bad news is…Theadora sent her away to make room for me." She cast her eyes downward, training them on the worn, braided carpet that lay over smooth oak floors.

"Oh, that," Carson replied dully. "You've nothing to be sorry about."

"That's kind of you to say," Hayley whispered gratefully. "And truly, I had nothing to do with it…at least not intentionally. But I know it was hard for you."

He stared at her dumbly. "You do?"

"Yes…Gabe told me."

Carson looked surprised. "Really? What did he tell you?"

Hayley hated to betray the boy's confidence, but she knew she had to continue, now that she'd begun. "That you were…smitten, but that there were circumstances that kept you from doing anything about it. I think he started to say something about Jenny, then stopped himself." She was unable to interpret the look on her companion's face. "Oh, please don't be angry with him!" she begged. "He was just…talking. You know how boys can be. And I think he realized he'd said too much. He wants very much to please you. You know that, don't you?"

"Yes, I know that." Carson's face broke into the smile that always accompanied any mention of his brother's name. "God only knows why. I haven't been nearly the parent he deserves." He sobered. "I haven't always done the right things for Gabe and Jenny," he admitted. "But I've never lied to them. And I won't lie to you." Hayley tore her eyes from the floor and met his gaze directly. "I had nothing to do with you being brought here, Hayley," he promised. "I thought there was something odd about Francine's sudden disappearance, but I didn't connect it to you at first. It wasn't until that day in the car that I realized there was something suspicious going on." He stood and began to pace the little room, tracing tiny circles around the brightly-colored carpet.

"I confronted Theadora, but she denied any ulterior motives. She claimed I was still upset about the affair between Evan and Jenny and told me to mind my own business. But the more I thought about it, the worse I felt. And then I remembered your name." He rubbed a rough hand over his face. "I don't know why it didn't strike me earlier. I guess it's because of the many years since anyone spoke about Jon. But last night, after I saw you and Simon together, I was cutting through the churchyard on my way back home when it all hit me."

Hayley remembered how he had knelt before her father's gravestone. "Tell me what you know…about my dad," Hayley asked timidly, unsure of whether she wanted to hear what he had to say.

"All right. But I—" Carson's eyes darted about the room, as if he were searching for something. "I don't know about you, but I need some more tea." He rescued his cup from the wobbly dining table and headed through a doorway at the far end of the room, into what Hayley assumed was the kitchen. "Would you like some?" he called back to her. "Kettle's already on the stove."

Hayley tried to keep her voice even. "No. No, thanks." She would give him no further opportunity for delay.

Whether Carson truly needed the tea to steady his nerves, or whether it simply helped him to have something to do with his hands, by the time he returned, he appeared much calmer. Hayley stole a glance at the strong-smelling, amber-colored liquid and thought that it *did* look wonderful. But she stubbornly refused to request a cup; nothing could induce her to prolong his explanation any further.

Braced by his tea, Carson dove right into his story. "Do you remember me telling you that before me, my father was the gardener at Newhaven?" Hayley nodded. "That was back in the sixties. Theadora's husband was still alive at the time, and he ruled the estate with an iron hand. You should have seen him and Theadora together."

"I gather they were a force to be reckoned with?"

The man snorted. "Ever hear of Evita Peron and her husband, Juan?"

"Mm-*hm*."

"Amateurs," Carson deadpanned. He acknowledged Hayley's expression of disbelief. "You think I'm kidding, but I'm not. David and Theodora were pretty brutal."

"If it was so bad, why did your parents stay?"

"That's a good question," Carson admitted. He considered for a moment before answering. "Things are...different here, Hayley. It's not like the States, where everyone moves about as he or she pleases. Here, there's family history. The Elliotts had been at Newhaven almost as long as the Harringtons. It was a lot to throw away." He glanced fondly around the cottage that had long been his family's home. "They had roots here. All their friends and family lived in town. My mother grew up in Harrington's Green. She eventually became close friends with Camilla, to the Harringtons' dismay." He looked smug. "Theodora and David had sent their daughter away to school and hoped to find her an appropriate match for marriage when she turned eighteen. Instead, through my mother, Camilla met Jon Buckman, my father's best friend from college, shortly after she returned from school."

Hayley drew her knees up under her chin, like a small child captivated by a romantic fairy tale. Only these characters weren't something from a book; they were the critical figures in her life story.

"The two lovebirds began to meet secretly at night inside the church." Carson drank deeply of his tea, then continued. "I imagine that added to the romance of it — clandestine meetings and all. The whole situation had a Romeo-and-Juliet feel to it. But no one thought much about it. After all, they were modern times. Some figured Jon and Camilla would just get over one another; others thought David and Theodora might eventually give in. No one imagined anything terrible would come of it...." His voice trailed off, and he seemed to weigh his next words. "It was about this time that the Venus disappeared."

Hayley felt the palms of her hands grow damp. This was too much. "The statue?" she whispered hoarsely.

"Mm." Carson raised his tea cup. "The statue."

"But...how?"

"By brute force, apparently...although the logistics are a little muzzy. It happened one day when there was a fete in the village. At that time, your father was working at the mill. The pay wasn't the greatest, and he was trying to save up enough to give him and your mother a decent start, so he often took on extra work. One day, to everyone's surprise, David Harrington started using him for odd jobs as well. Your mother was thrilled. I think even Jon hoped he was coming around." A look of anger crossed Carson's face. "On this one particular day, David Harrington had sent him in to London to pick up some auto parts. Everyone else was at the festival. Later that night, it was discovered that the statue had been stolen away. Eventually everyone's alibis seemed to be confirmed — except your father's." By this time, Carson was shaking so badly he had to place his rattling cup and saucer on the floor.

"He had returned from London later than was expected, due to the fact that the parts weren't ready when he arrived at the shop. When the constables started their investigation, Jon gave them his explanation, and they interviewed the clerk at the auto repair shop." Carson paused. "The stories didn't match."

Hayley stared at him, trying to believe what she was hearing. Her father? *Jon Buckman?* Accused of art theft?

"He was set up?"

Carson sighed. "Exactly."

She tried to imagine her parents' reaction to such circumstances. "What did my mother do?"

"I heard she was furious. Told her parents she wouldn't be controlled, that she loved Jon and had promised to marry him as soon as she was able to without her parents' permission." Carson spoke with a passion. "Unfortunately, Theadora and David didn't exactly take to being put in their place. Their daughter's stubbornness only fueled their anger, and they decided to get rid of Jon once and for all.

"You see, art theft is a very serious business, and this wasn't just any old statue. It was rumored to be a piece done by Joseph Nollekens — you've heard of him, I suppose?" Hayley shook her head. "He was a man of extraordinary talent; one of England's greatest sculptors. No one knew for sure if he had created the piece, although I suspect tests could confirm it today if the thing were still around. It seems logical: the style was consistent with his, and Nollekens was known for his love of sculpting goddesses. There are a number of surviving examples: Diana, Minerva, Juno — and several others of Venus, if I'm not mistaken. If the statue were authentic, it was worth a great deal of money, indeed.

"Everyone knew Jon didn't do it, but David was determined that he should be sentenced for the crime. Camilla was devastated. The clerk had obviously been paid off. It was certain that Jon would be sent away. There seemed to be no escape." Hayley tried to imagine what her parents might have felt, but the situation seemed too incredible to grasp.

"Jon hadn't yet been arrested," Carson told her, "although

the police were gathering evidence, and it was only a matter of time. Then, three days after the statue's disappearance, Jon Buckman disappeared. David and Theadora were beside themselves with joy. His action simply proved their theory. Two days later, a country lad reported that a body bearing Jon's personal effects had washed ashore down river. It was Reverend Archer who identified and claimed the body. Camilla insisted upon burying him at the estate. Her parents finally agreed, hoping to put the incident behind them once and for all. It was a small ceremony. Only Camilla, my parents, and the reverend attended. Camilla refused to allow her parents to come.

"And the incident was not put behind them at all. Camilla kept herself locked in her room. She wouldn't speak to either one of them. Then one day, she suddenly disappeared. All she left was a note telling them she could not live under the same roof as those who had conspired against her love. David and Theadora tried desperately to find her, searching all over England, France — any place they thought she might have gone. Yet they never saw Camilla Harrington again."

Silence fell heavily between them. Then Carson grinned.

"But *I* did."

"Wha —" Hayley leaned eagerly over the arm of her chair. "What are you saying? *You* saw my mother? When?"

"Hm." Carson scratched his chin thoughtfully. "I'd say. Now was it? Yes, indeed." Hayley watched him innocently, completely unaware of what was to come. Carson's face broke into a grin.

"I'd say it was right about the time I first saw you!"

Seventeen

⤜✧⤛

Sweet Love of youth, forgive, if I forget thee.
Emily Bronte, *Remembrance*

Carson's eyes glinted mischievously.

"Me!" Hayley fought back nervous laughter. "You're just making that up!"

"No, seriously," he insisted, his face the picture of sincerity. "It was several years after the statue disappeared. Our fathers were best friends, remember? They kept in touch by post via London. What?" He waggled his bushy eyebrows at her. "You didn't think your father actually died in the river, did you?"

"No, *I did not think my father died in the river!*" Hysterical giggles threatened to rise from Hayley's throat.

"I should think not!" Carson said haughtily. He forced himself to turn back to the subject. "At the time, I think I must have been about four. Jenny hadn't been born yet. I remember how excited my parents were about seeing Jon and Camilla again. You were just a bit of a thing. Maybe two, at most. What are you now?" Carson looked at her as if measuring her in years. "Twenty-three, twenty-four?" He shrugged. "I don't remember much about the stay, although I do recall that you followed me around every place I went. You were quite taken with me. But then, who could blame you?" He smirked.

"Ha, ha." Hayley registered his attempt at humor, but her voice held no real mirth. "You're telling me we've actually met before?" She shuddered. "Okay, this is all too *Twilight Zone*-ish for me."

Carson chuckled. "I can't believe you don't remember. You adored me."

"Sorry." Staring into his laughing eyes, Hayley wondered if her subconscious remembered what her conscious did not. From the beginning, she had felt in her soul that Carson was a man she could trust, despite her confusion. "So what happened during the visit?"

"I think they talked about your parents coming back to England, but it still wasn't safe. The funny thing is, the statue never turned up anywhere. Theadora put feelers out on the black market — or at least she *said* she did. But it never surfaced. That just added fuel to the theory that Jon had taken it but had died before being able to sell it. Jon and Camilla decided they could be safe only if they stayed in America. That was the last our parents ever saw of one another."

Hayley clasped clammy palms together to still their shaking. "That's so...sad."

"It is," Carson agreed. "But not as sad as if Jon had been sentenced to prison. Your parents did what they had to do, Hayley," he assured her gently.

"But not to *tell* me...," she protested weakly.

"They did what they thought was best." The words were right, but Hayley was not convinced.

"But what does it all mean?" She sighed miserably. "And what do the Harringtons want of me now?"

"Don't worry little one." He smiled at her fondly, as if seeing the adoring child he once knew. Resolutely, he placed both feet firmly on the floor, stretched his lanky frame to its full six feet, three inches, and pulled her up to stand beside him. "Obviously those rotters are up to something. But they seem to have forgotten one thing that I haven't." He grinned like a mischievous grammar school boy and whispered in her ear:

"*You're* a Harrington, too."

Carson then proposed a follow-up visit with the Reverend Archer. "After all," he reasoned, "he's the one who supposedly identified your father's body. He must have been in on the whole thing."

"Shall I come clean?" Hayley wondered aloud, sounding like the villain in a dime-store detective novel. "Tell him who I am? Confess everything?"

"I don't know, 'Mugsy.'" Carson smirked. "Why don't we just see what he has to say first?"

Too worked up to laugh in return, Hayley simply nodded. As they headed side by side toward the chapel, Carson made an effort to slow his pace, while Hayley attempted to lengthen her stride. As a result, they were able to match each other's steps fairly well and strolled in companionable silence. The quiet was comforting. When in the presence of someone she did not know well, Hayley normally felt compelled to make small talk. But after all they had shared, it would seem almost irreverent to engage in idle chatter. Nor did Hayley want to continue just yet with their in-depth analysis. For now, it felt right just to share a moment of peace.

As they entered the chapel, Hayley was impressed once again by the quality and beauty of the medieval architecture.

High overhead, the ceiling stretched like a great gray sky. In contrast to the morning's tension, Hayley experienced a feeling something like peace as she stepped into the structure's cool, still air.

"Reverend Archer?" Carson's voice echoed eerily in the empty space. His ungainly feet clomped against the stone floor as he approached the chancel. "Reverend?" The silence was unbroken by reply. He turned to Hayley with a lop-sided grin that seemed meant to offer comfort. "Wait here," he directed, then retraced his steps to the narthex.

Hayley watched his retreating figure fondly, then turned her architect's eye back to the front of the church. During her visit with the reverend she had longed for an opportunity to examine the relief more carefully but had been hesitant to ask. The last thing she wanted was for the old man to read deeper meaning into her simple appreciation of art.

Quietly, although she was essentially alone, Hayley tiptoed past the baptismal font and drew close to the impressive carved image on the wall. She smiled at the sound of Carson's voice behind her, bouncing impudently off the vaulted ceiling, then focused her full attention to the detailed relief of The Last Judgment.

Right away, Hayley found herself slipping back into the patterns she had developed while taking art history back in college. First, her eyes swept over the image as a whole, taking in the color of the stone, the depth of the lines, the quality of form. Next, she drank in the chorus of details. The proportion of the figures. The liveliness of expression. The element of realism.

Based in part, as far as Hayley could discern, on the depiction at the Sistine Chapel, the piece focused on the central figure of Christ, surrounded by angels and a multitude of souls rising forth from the grave to receive judgment. Just as in Michelangelo's famous work, the relief portrayed many of the dead draped in their burial shrouds; others were fully clothed. In some cases, only the bones had risen; a number of figures were only partially covered with flesh.

Many of the dead wore expressions that were unreadable. Some gazed about with heavy eyes, as if surprised to find themselves suddenly wakened. Dozens reached out hopefully toward heaven; others stared into space, their faces betraying unspeakable fear.

At that moment, Hayley was stirred beyond a simple appreciation of art by a feeling so powerful, it overwhelmed her mind and senses. *This is true.* As sure as she knew her own name, she recognized that the judgment — the very one depicted in such graphic images — would one day come. She was overcome by the sudden realization that the inner battle she was waging was not simply one of ideas and ideals. She was confronted not by issues of philosophy, but by a decision regarding the future of her soul.

For centuries, artists had tried to reinforce what God had told man. The words were carved in stone beneath the judgment scene:

Then will appear in heaven the sign that heralds the Son of Man. All the peoples of the world will make lamentation, and they will see the Son of Man coming on the clouds of heaven with great power and glory.... Therefore you must also be ready; for the Son of man is coming at an hour you do not expect.

— St. Matthew 24:30, 44

"'All the peoples of the world will make lamentation....'" Hayley shivered. When that day came, she did not want to be lamenting. No matter how valid were her complaints regarding a specific church or the church as a whole, she suddenly knew she could not find the answers she needed by running from God.

But wasn't her struggle understandable? She wanted to believe in God. Yet much of what she had seen in church seemed pat, premeditated...without soul. Everyone had expected Hayley to accept without question the justice of her parents' deaths. In reaction to her expressed doubts, many of her family's friends had recoiled in horror. "Don't question it, Hayley. It was God's will. You can't doubt God." But how could she *not* question it? Would she be human if she did not?

Ever since the fire, Hayley had felt disconnected from God. She imagined he was angry at her for her failure to attend church during college — and had punished her by letting her parents die. She determined that he had withdrawn his protection when she stopped praying after her parents' deaths. She'd blamed him for expecting her to be perfect in her acceptance of her loss.

Hayley had believed it was her right to hurt, that it was normal to feel angry. But in the time of her most intense grief, the message she had received at her church was exactly the opposite. That's what had driven her away in the end. It seemed to Hayley that God was demanding a response she could not offer; she imagined him trying to regulate her feelings. It was at that point she decided to take back control: when she determined that God did not love her as she was — questions, doubts, and all. Why couldn't God have allowed Hayley her feelings?

Suddenly, Hayley felt a stirring in her heart: a feeling of peace greater even than that which she had experienced upon entering the church. No vision appeared before her eyes; she heard no words in her head. But she was certain God was speaking to her when she understood at the core of her being that all along, he'd done exactly what she had wished: Allowed her to work it through in her own time.

He had not forced himself upon her. Yet he remained at her side, from time to time gently whispering her name. He had reached out to her in moments she did not expect his touch. Once, Hayley had imagined she heard him in the laughter of a friend. Many times she had seen him in the gentle unfolding of a rose. She had felt him in the soft caress of a summer breeze.

He knew that she was hurting. And he had been waiting.

He'd waited for her in the back of the church after her parents' funeral. He'd accompanied her to the school library and waited for her in her tiny apartment each night. He'd even waited for her in Newhaven's bountiful gardens; in the last week, she'd caught numerous glimpses of him in the circle of death and new life.

Today, God had waited for her in an isolated country chapel. He had called to her from a piece of stone. And somehow, Hayley had finally managed to hear his voice.

Overcome by passionate feelings she could not name, Hayley dropped to her knees and lost herself in wordless prayer, offering her heart to the relentlessly loving Father who had never given up in his pursuit of her. It was there, at Jesus' feet, that Carson found her kneeling, tears streaming down her cheeks.

At the sound of his footsteps, she turned.

"Sorry." Carson hesitated, his face filled with compassion. "Would you like me to go?"

"No, no. It's all right." Hayley reached for his hand, and Carson drew her to her feet. His touch was gentle, reassuring. The eyes that saw much seemed to read her soul. Hayley drank in his expression with a deep sense of gratitude, realizing that he understood perfectly. An arrow of pleasure pierced her heart, and she delighted in the thrill of being known. "Did you find the reverend?" She tried to keep her voice light, even as her heart began to recognize the depth of feeling stirred by Carson's support.

Her companion's face split into a wide grin. "No. But I found something even better!"

As she wiped away her tears, Hayley noticed the mischievous new glint in her companion's eyes. She laughed. "All right, then. I'll bite. What's better than finding the reverend?"

"How about finding your parents?" Carson said smugly.

"Excuse me?" Hayley put a finger to her ear and wiggled it, clearing the passage of imaginary water. "I thought you just said finding my parents."

Her companion gave her a self-satisfied nod. "Exactly. There was one thing I forgot to mention. You see, my mother was a bit of a romantic, and she had a tendency to ramble on about the different couples she knew. Of course, Jon and Camilla were her favorites. I remember she got all sentimental one day when she was reminiscing about your parents' courtship and how everything had to be kept such a secret. Naturally, as a boy, I couldn't have cared less.

"Until she got to the part about the hiding place." He wagged his eyebrows playfully. "I already told you that your parents used to meet here at the chapel. But the part I left out was that they would often leave letters for one another under a loose stone in the narthex. I tried and tried to find that secret spot when I was a boy, and I never did," Carson told her wryly. "But just now, I thought I'd give it one more attempt. I knew it couldn't be under the floor, or I would have found it as a lad. So this time, I tried up higher. There weren't many possibilities. But I did discover a loose piece of stone in one corner...." He paused for dramatic effect. "And I found this underneath."

Carson had been holding one arm behind him; he now drew his hand forward and proffered a small, yellowed envelope. Hayley's mind fell blank, and the room seemed to tilt. Clutching Carson's arm to steady herself, she made her way to the foremost pew and eased her shaking body down onto the polished wood.

My parents.... There was no name on the envelope; clearly, none had been needed. Hayley had hoped to reestablish some sort of connection with her parents; she now held in her hands a fragment of their past. Carson let her hand drop and stepped away discreetly, allowing her the opportunity to read the message semi-privately, yet remaining a few short steps away.

With hands that shook so badly she was afraid she might rip the paper, Hayley unfolded the note and read through a haze of tears:

Dearest Jonathan,

Today, for the last time, I watched you wander about the Green... leaving behind the sweat and camaraderie of the mill, laughing at some dreadful joke of Caleb's...wanting so desperately to say my good-byes, yet knowing that one mis-spoken word could mean imprisonment.

How I wish you were not suffering because of your love for me! When I think of all you have endured at my father's hands — the insults, the accusations — and all you have yet to bear, including separation from your friends and home, I wish for your sake that we had never met.

Yet for myself, I cannot desire any such thing. I confess, my heart is greedy and thinks only of itself. Even in the midst of turmoil, it finds pleasure in knowing that you love me enough to sacrifice everything for a new beginning.

Our future begins tonight.

I do not know if you will return to the chapel before this evening. I will proceed as we have planned, unless given the word to do otherwise by Galen or the reverend.

May the God who brought us together keep you safe until I am in your arms once more.

— Cami

Hayley devoured the words with her eyes. Her mother's gentle voice seemed to leap from the crumbling page.

There was no greater gift she could have received. The house fire that had taken her parents' lives had also destroyed all that they owned. There was little left that could evoke memories of home and family. But here, suddenly, was a perfect record of her parents' love.

Like every child, Hayley had taken for granted her parents' feelings for one another. In truth, they were more genuinely affectionate than the parents of her friends. But Hayley lived with them day in and day out. They were, at times, cross with one another…although they always made up before much time passed.

But now she realized that they weren't just a man and a woman who had chosen to live together and raise a child; they were lovers whose passionate feelings had matured and deepened over time. And here in her hands was tangible evidence of their love.

Carson approached slowly and sat beside her on the hard wood. He searched her face with questioning eyes, and with trembling fingers, Hayley placed the precious letter in his hands.

She watched as he read. His eyes darted quickly across the page. At one point, his brow wrinkled. Then the soft curve of his strong mouth turned gently upward. He turned to Hayley and enveloped her in a look of great tenderness. Silently, they gazed at one another, their eyes expressing emotions their voices could not.

Carson leaned forward and took Hayley's chin in his work-roughened hand. His lips parted, as if to speak.…

"Hullo! There you are!" The massive chapel door fell shut with a bang as Gabriel pounded breathlessly toward them. "I've been looking for you everywhere! You won't believe the row they're having on the terrace!" He paused for a split-second to catch his breath. "You two had better come quick!"

Eighteen

❦

This is a rotten argument, but it should be good enough
for their lordships on a hot summer afternoon.
Anonymous annotation to ministerial brief,
said to have been read inadvertently in the House of Lords

Gabriel hopped from one foot to another, unable to control his impatience. "Come on," he urged. "It was just getting good!"

"What happened?" Reluctantly, Carson pulled away from Hayley and dragged his lanky frame off the pew.

"I don't know what started it," Gabe admitted. He grabbed Hayley by the wrist and started pulling her toward the door. "But I could hear the row clear out to the formal garden, so I went to in-ves-ti-gate." He said the word with relish. Hayley recognized the familiar Elliott glint in his eye. "Simon was coming down upon Evan about Hayley! I thought he might thump his nose!" he said cheerfully. "Hurry up. It's a jolly good show!" He took off at a run with Hayley and Carson at his heels.

❦

By the time they arrived, the argument was in full swing. The beautiful wrought-iron table was piled high with tea and scones that sat untouched. On either side stood one of the two Harrington brothers. Evan, as usual, had taken center stage and was roaring something about brotherly loyalty. But the gentleness of Simon's demeanor seemed to have given way to quiet determination. His back was straight; he met Evan's glare with steady eyes. He seemed unlikely to back down.

"What exactly are you saying, then, Brother?" Evan growled at the younger man.

"I'm saying that you and Theadora had no right deceiving her like that," Simon accused. "We're talking about a person here. She had a right to know. Besides, she was bound to find out eventually. Why don't you use your head?"

"Why don't *you?*" Evan leered. "You think I don't know what this is about? Here you are, the white knight in shining armor, protecting the damsel in distress. How knotty can you be, Simon? You've already got one woman. What do you think you're about, courting a second?"

From behind them came the sound of a strangled moan. Hayley's eyes caught a hint of green sage. Horrified, she turned to see Isabelle standing hidden in the shadows. The woman's eyes rolled back under heavy lids, but she did not speak. Slim, tanned arms crossed over the front of her body, as if protecting against physical blows. She made no attempt to move.

Simon took a half-hearted step toward her. "Isabelle, he didn't mean —" His eyes flew open wide at the sight of Hayley, standing at the edge of the terrace, and behind her a grim-looking Carson and a grinning Gabe.

"Hayley! I —" He leveled a glance at his brother. "Not a

word, Evan," he ordered in a low voice. It was the first time Hayley had heard either one call the other by name. Then, to her surprise, Simon ignored Isabelle's obvious distress and came to stand by her side. He took her hand gently. "My dear, please don't be angry. I told him you had sent me packing as well, but my brother is incredibly jealous. Just ignore him —"

"Oh, you'd like that, wouldn't you?" Evan snarled. "There's nothing you'd love more than for us all to turn our backs and let you chase after her. Meanwhile, *Brother*, what you've forgotten is the fact that she's here to finish what her father began. She's after the statue, and she'll have it, too, if you keep mooning about. She'll wait until the rest of us are occupied. Something tells me that *you* won't be difficult to distract," he cracked. "And then she'll send in her lackeys — probably those two behind her there. What?" He laughed at Hayley's look of shock. "I suppose you think they have no ulterior motives? They want the same thing we all do, including *you*," he insisted. "The question is, whom shall you trust? *Those* bloody fools," he nodded toward Carson and Gabe, "or your family?" He stepped close and curled his lips suggestively. "We still could be kissing cousins, you know."

Hayley hadn't even a chance to react; in seconds, both Simon and Evan were at her side.

"That's *enough*. You're pushing too far, Brother," Simon warned, fists clenched at his side.

"And what are you going to do about it, *Brother?*" Evan taunted.

"I'll dust your jacket —"

"Go on. Try it," the older Harrington returned.

Before Hayley could even open her mouth to protest, the

two had begun flailing wildly at one another. Simon seemed strong enough and was fueled by anger. But he was clearly no match for his older brother. Within seconds, Evan had seized the advantage and was pummeling Simon for all he was worth.

"Carson…do something!" she gasped.

The gardener looked like he was inclined to let the two men destroy one another. But, sensing her distress, he moved to break up the fight.

"All right, all right," Carson shouted, pulling the bigger man off the top. "Clear off, you two. We've had enough of this tom-lad bout of yours." Then, when they would not stop, "Give over, I say!" He wedged a bony elbow into Evan's side, looking pleased as he did so. Seconds later, Simon caught Carson with a blow to the ribs. *"Oof!"* he protested. All traces of his good humor were gone. He looked as if he might be tempted to throw a few jabs himself. "All right, I'm flipping mad now! Come on, you blithering idiots. *Give over,"* he grunted.

Several knee jabs, full punches, and eye gouges later, the men were separated, but it was clear that Simon had borne the worst of the fight. Evan was sweating mildly, and his neatly-pressed suit was a mass of untucked wrinkles. Carson's hair stood crazily on end, and he sported a rapidly-swelling lip, but blood actually dripped from Simon's nose, and it appeared as though his right eye might balloon shut.

Panting from the physical exertion, Carson threw a dubious look in Evan's direction. "Funny," he muttered suspiciously. "If I didn't know better, I'd say for a moment there you were aiming at me and not your brother."

A snort of derisive laughter was Evan's only reply.

Hayley expected Isabelle to rush forward to Simon's aid, but the woman remained in her corner, looking neither shocked nor alarmed. Hayley tried to catch her eye, to indicate that she should assist her fiancé, but Isabelle seemed doggedly determined to avoid her gaze.

Sighing in frustration, Hayley grabbed a napkin from the table, doused it in ice water, and proceeded to mop up the tiny scarlet river running down Simon's face.

Her patient submitted gratefully to her ministrations. "Thank you," he said quietly when she was finished. He made no move to touch her, but the look in his eyes communicated tremendous depth of feeling. Despite her anger, Hayley offered a tiny smile to the man who had sacrificed peace with his brother in order to defend her honor.

"All right! That's bought it!" Carson exploded. He could contain his fury no longer. "As far as I'm concerned, the two of you can have one another. I'm done with you." Shoving an iron chair roughly from his path, he stalked away in a rage.

Too spent to argue, too disappointed to explain, there was nothing Hayley could do but sadly watch him go.

Nineteen

*Gude grant that thou may aye inherit / Thy mither's person,
grace, an' merit, / An' thy poor worthless daddy's spirit,
Without his failins; / 'Twill please me mair to see and hear o't.*
Robert Burns, *The Poet's Welcome*

Ash-toned stone lay cold and lifeless beneath the warmth of
Hayley's hands. Pressing the rough pads of her fingers
against a layer of loose dirt and pebbles, she grunted and
hoisted her body up onto the pedestal. Then, with an awkward
twist of her small frame, she worked herself into a sitting position, letting her heavy boots dangle.

Her eyes surveyed the surrounding carpet of green and the
yew-bough ceiling draped high overhead, but immediately, and
without intention, she found her attention drawn back to the
heavy gouge-marks beneath her outspread hands. The cuts
were deep and wide. Clearly they had been caused by some
man-operated machine. Hayley closed her eyes and tried to
imagine the thief — or thieves — tackling the difficult task,
but no amount of effort could bring her to impose her father's
face on the mysterious figure.

With the exception of a small brown wren in the branches
above, she was alone in the garden. Yet, the solitude failed to

comfort Hayley. Despite the stillness, she could still hear the echo of angry voices from several hours earlier.

I wish I'd never come. It would be better not to know. If only she'd finished her degree back in the States. She'd be at some nice city park or private mansion or southern plantation, minding her own business…far from the conniving cousins, vengeful socialite, power-hungry grandmother, and jealous superior who were tearing her heart in two.

A figure appeared at the edge of the clearing, interrupting her musings. Irritated, but not surprised by the intrusion, Hayley blinked in recognition, then turned her face away.

The woman approached with a stride that was slow, but determined. "It's terribly rude to ignore someone, Hayley." Theadora's words were cutting, but her tone lacked its typical harshness. "I believe it would have caused your mother great distress to see you snub me in this manner." Her small feet shuffled resolutely across the soft grass.

"Well," Hayley shot back sullenly. "You certainly know a lot about a woman you haven't seen in twenty-six years." She pushed her slumped figure upright with a quick, jerking motion, drawing blood as she scraped her hands against the stone.

Theadora's black eyes snapped with anger, but she did not rise to the bait. "I remember a few things," she said a bit stiffly as she came to a halt.

Despite her anger, Hayley felt awkward sitting comfortably while the elderly woman was forced to stand. She glanced around the clearing, but if benches were ever positioned around the statue, they had been removed in the years since its disappearance. For a moment, Hayley considered hopping off the pedestal, then decided that Theadora's well-being was none of her concern and determined to remain just where she was. As if to punctuate her resolution, she rebelliously kicked her Doc Martens against the statue's base.

Theadora eyed her disapprovingly but managed to bite back her displeasure. "I've just come from speaking with the Elliott boy. He told me about the confrontation on the terrace."

Hayley grunted in reply while continuing to pound her feet against the stone.

Although disdain was written all over Theadora's face, she spoke with measured civility. "I apologize for the behavior of my brother's grandchildren. They haven't any manners at all, I fear." The gesture was ruined by the pointed look she gave Hayley's thumping feet.

"Gee," Hayley replied bitterly, thumping with enthusiasm. "I guess I fit right into the family, then."

Theadora nervously folded and unfolded her hands. "Young lady, you needn't be so *acid.* I am, after all, your grandmother. Your own flesh and blood. I hardly see —"

"That's right!" Hayley exploded, her sullen features transformed into a mask of anger. "You hardly see *anything,* except what you choose! Well, I'll tell you what *I* see." She glared at the woman whose daughter had given her life, but she could see nothing but a bitter, controlling matriarch. "I see a woman who lied to me, bringing me thousands of miles from home under completely false pretenses. I see someone who has, ever since my arrival, tried to belittle and intimidate me. I see a mother who tried to come between the daughter she supposedly cared for and the man her daughter loved." Her eyes narrowed. "Feel free to stop me if I'm missing something here."

"What you are missing," Theadora sniffed haughtily, "is a true interpretation of facts." Then her tone softened, and she seemed almost to wheedle. "No one lied to you, Hayley. I brought you here so I could have the chance to get to know the granddaughter I never knew I had."

"Oh, please!" Hayley let out a humorless laugh. "Like I'm supposed to believe that? I know you have other reasons."

The white-haired woman looked irritated. "Such as?"

"Well…I don't know, *exactly*," Hayley admitted reluctantly, her kicking abandoned as she searched her mind for the proper words. "But upon more than one occasion, Evan and Isabelle each made it clear that you expect to use me for your own purposes." She gave Theadora a cold stare. "You might as well know, I won't be any help to you at all. My —" She nearly said "parents," then remembered her advantage and caught herself just in time. "My mother rarely spoke of England and never *once* mentioned Newhaven. I don't have any information that can help you find your crummy old statue, so you might as well just leave me out of it."

Theadora shifted her weight from one foot to the other. "I'm sure I don't know what you're talking about." She sounded offended.

"I'm *sure*," Hayley mimicked dryly and resumed her kicking.

"Now see here!" Theadora's voice rose in pitch. "I will not allow you to use that tone with me. You forget to whom you are speaking!" She held herself regally, her self-importance showing. "You disappoint me, young lady. I had hoped to find that you had taken after your mother. Camilla was sweet and gentle and always polite. She never raised her voice to her father, or to me —"

"Perhaps if she could have, she wouldn't have been forced to run away!" Hayley challenged.

Theadora's face turned pale. "I see you take after Jonathan. Camilla's father and I respected his spirit, but not his character. I am sorry to see that you have inherited his character."

"Thank you," Hayley muttered through clenched teeth. "I take that as a compliment."

"Really, Hayley," Theadora sounded exasperated. "Must you *incite* an argument? I do not intend to 'use' you for anything. I hadn't any ulterior motives, and I resent your implication that I had."

"If you're so innocent," Hayley challenged, "then why weren't you honest with me? Why all the secrecy?"

Her composure broken, Theadora began to pace. "My motives weren't as sinister as you seem determined to believe. It was simple, really. When I realized who you were, I knew that I was faced with one of two situations. Either you had no knowledge about the family connection, and luck had brought you to me, or..." She hesitated. "Or you had an agenda of your own."

"Me!" Hayley's eyes were filled with fury. "An agenda? Of all the *ridiculous*—"

"Don't interrupt!" Theadora snapped, matching Hayley's ire. She took a breath and made an effort to collect herself. "Initially," she explained, "I was suspicious. Especially after I caught you spying on me in the gardens." Hayley's face burned red-hot, but she made no attempt to clear herself. "But I eventually decided you were up to no harm."

"After you spent all those days in the garden, grilling me!" Hayley accused, a hint of pain creeping into her voice. "You deliberately provoked me," she realized incredulously. *"Didn't* you? What, exactly, were you trying to prove?"

"I was simply...observing your reactions to various situations." Theadora spoke with an air of resigned patience, as if her intentions should have been obvious to Hayley. "And I was pleased to discover that you did not, at any point, respond toward me with animosity. That's when I decided your coming here was nothing more than a happy coincidence." She seemed to think Hayley should feel relieved by this revelation.

"Happy?" Hayley could not believe her ears. *"Happy?* That really takes the cake. Do you have any idea how *miserable* you people have made me? Isabelle, trying to scare me with her nasty little note. You, first treating me like Mata Hari, now trying to play father to my prodigal son. And I don't know *which* one of you cranks has been following me, but —"

"Following you?" Theadora's face appeared blank, then took on shadows as understanding dawned on her. It was clear to Hayley that the woman was not responsible for setting someone on her trail; it was just as obvious that she knew who was behind the harassment. "I did not realize that was the case. However, I can assure you that you will not be bothered further."

Hayley realized that there was *no one* with whom her grandmother got along well. But the look on Theadora's face was so venomous, it could have been triggered by only one individual. "Evan?" Hayley ventured. But no answer was needed.

"He's thought all along that you'd come back to find the statue," Theadora admitted, keeping her eyes level with Hayley's. "I've no doubt he's keeping tabs on you, to see if you'll give away any clue to its hidden location."

"But that's absurd!" Hayley protested. "Even if I *did* know something about it, how on earth does he expect one woman to sneak away with a — what, a four-five-foot marble statue? Has he lost his mind?"

"That, my dear," Theadora sniffed, "is a rhetorical question. I doubt that logic plays a terribly large role in Evan's thinking."

"But —" Hayley protested weakly.

"But nothing," Theadora assured her. "Evan will not bother you any longer. I'll see to it. He's a selfish lad, but I doubt he means any real harm." The words sounded sincere enough, but Hayley could not shake the feeling that Theadora was trying to convince not only her granddaughter, but herself as well.

The younger woman did not accept the offer of protection, but neither did she reject it. For a moment, the two stared at each other amid an emotion-charged silence. Finally Hayley broke the quiet with the question that was burning within her heart.

"Why wouldn't you accept my father?"

Theadora met the question in Hayley's eyes, then let her gaze drop to the verdant carpet beneath her expensively-booted feet. "Of course I don't expect you to understand, child. Naturally, you feel a bond with your father; I could not have expected otherwise. No doubt, you feel anger about his death — perhaps you even blame us for the fact that you never had an opportunity to meet him."

Hayley moved her lips as if to speak, but no sound came forth.

"I don't approve of the fact that your mother conceived you outside of marriage," Theadora went on. "Although I suppose I'm glad, for your sake, that she managed to hide the fact and give you your father's name. Had I suspected that you existed, we would have tried even harder to find her — to find *you*." Her voice was unexpectedly tender. "This family has experienced enough pain. When Camilla left, I swore to keep the rest of the family together, no matter the cost. That's why I still allow Evan and Simon at Newhaven. I've even put up with that scatty little fiancée…because I could not bear for there to be another Harrington lost." Hayley took in the woman's slumped shoulders and tired, yellowed eyes. It indeed looked as though loss had taken its toll upon the lady of the manor.

"I don't know how to explain a parent's motivation," Theadora continued. "I believe it is something you cannot understand until you have experienced it for yourself. All I can tell you is that your grandfather and I wanted only the best for Camilla." She spoke with quiet pride. "We made mistakes which we later regretted, but at the time, we did what we thought was right."

Hayley still could not accept her answer. "You did what you thought was right *for you*," she insisted bitterly. "The only thing you *regretted* was the fact that you lost your daughter. You didn't believe you had done anything wrong. You still don't."

"Hayley —"

But the fiery brunette was truly wound up now. "You wanted to control, not to love, my mother," Hayley spoke passionately. "And you aren't any different today than you were then. You've tried to control me ever since you learned I was alive! You manipulated circumstances to bring me here; you submitted me to your sneaky little tests. I don't think I can believe a word you say!" she spat out.

The sharp black gaze seemed to dull before Hayley's eyes. Her last words seemed to take the fight out of Theadora's argument. The older woman sighed heavily; she looked beaten, like she had on the day Hayley found her in her library. "I suppose there is no reason why you should." She turned away in defeat, the slump to her shoulders even greater than when she had arrived.

Hayley watched her go and a flood of sadness swept over her heart. Twice, she nearly raised her voice to stop the woman; twice, she stopped herself as she remembered the suffering Theadora had caused her parents. She could not forget what the woman had done. Nor could she forgive. Not that there was any reason to. Theadora had mentioned regret, but not once had she asked for forgiveness.

The conclusion seemed cold, and Hayley felt ashamed. An annoying question nagged at the fringes of her thoughts: *Is an apology a valid prerequisite for forgiveness?* Theadora's suffering was evident, and Hayley was clearly a cause of her pain.

But it's not my fault. I didn't cause her guilt. And I never asked to be a Harrington.

At first, the thought cheered Hayley a bit. She *was* the real wounded party here. She hadn't asked for this. Although… Hayley was forced to admit, she *had* cried out to God a number of times in the past years, asking him why he had left her alone. Now she had more relatives than she knew what to do with…or wanted. Her spiritual cynicism returned. Was this God's idea of a joke? Her mind filled with the memory of her gently moving experience in the chapel, and Hayley felt strangely comforted. The God who had called out to her was not a God of games. It was true: he hadn't prevented her parents' deaths. But he *had* given her the strength to survive the loss. And now he had allowed her — through extraordinary circumstances — to find those relatives who remained.

Hayley stared at the spot where, moments before, Theadora had stood. If things kept going the way they were going, she would soon lose them all again.

And this time, if she were not mistaken, it would be for good.

Twenty

✦

An wilt thou leave me thus? / Say nay, say nay, for shame.
Sir Thomas Wyatt, *An Appeal*

Hayley dug her fingers deep into the chalky Chiltern soil. Although she'd been mixing for a full fifteen minutes, the texture still was not quite right. Soft, tiny granules slid between forefinger and thumb. "Needs more compost," she muttered to no one in particular.

"Well, you're in the right place," someone in particular replied. "We've plenty of it." A long, thin shadow fell across her shoulders.

"Oh. Hello." Hayley looked up and stared into Carson's eyes. "It's you," she said stupidly.

He did not acknowledge her lack of grace. "What are you planting?" The words conveyed carefully-measured interest, but his eyes darted about nervously, touching upon his scuffed shoes, the oval of Hayley's face, the gently-sloped horizon — everything but the plot of earth beneath her hands.

"Nothing." Hayley sighed, a little louder than she intended. "I just had to keep busy, and I saw you had this section marked off for a new bed."

"That was thoughtful."

Hayley couldn't think of how he expected her to answer, so turned back to her task. The shadow retreated, re-advanced, then repeated its actions in a dance of indecision. Finally it stopped, and Carson knelt beside her.

"I shouldn't have lost my temper earlier," he admitted quietly.

Hayley kept digging.

"I — uh — may have overreacted a bit," he tried again.

Hayley concentrated on her mixing. She wanted to forgive him. But the idea of giving in, just so he could mistrust her yet again, seemed too painful to be worth the risk. She kept her voice light. "You know, you can't just go around assuming people are having affairs."

Carson paused. "I know." He sounded genuinely remorseful.

Hayley stabbed viciously at the earth with her wooden trowel. "Hmmph." She acknowledged his acknowledgment. "Well, it wasn't the first time you'd jumped to conclusions where I was concerned. You must not think much of me. Not that I care *what* you think." She forced herself to act cool, aloof.

"Hayley, don't." Carson sounded grim. "Please?" He reached out and covered her mud-caked fingers with his own. She struggled to keep them stiff and unresponsive. *"Hayley."* With the hand that remained dirt-free, he gently tilted her face toward his. She tried not to meet his eyes. "Don't go away. I'm *sorry*. Truly I am." His voice was gentle, and for a moment Hayley was almost swayed. Then, "It's just those two bloody idiots!" Carson burst out. "They make me so flipping mad! Especially when it comes to —" He broke off, realizing he was making things worse. "I just don't trust those two," he continued, more calmly. "And I value you too much to let you get caught up with them."

Hayley bristled. "Since when is it up to you to decide who I get 'caught up with'? Besides which, you seem to have forgotten, I can't help being mixed up with them even if I want to. They're relatives. *Distant* relatives, I admit. But relatives nonetheless...at least of Theadora's. No doubt I'll be dealing with them for the rest of my life." The thought was dismaying, but Hayley kept that feeling to herself.

Carson leaned forward eagerly. "Not if you leave Newhaven."

Hayley stared back at him. "Excuse me? You know I can't leave. I have to finish my internship —"

"Oh, don't be scatty!" Carson scoffed. "You know as well as I that your school would let you off the hook if you explained what happened. You can finish up your credits elsewhere."

Hayley sat back on work-calloused heels. She continued, more determinedly, "I'm not a quitter, Carson. You should know me better than that. Besides, my internship isn't the only issue here. I have a score to settle with Theadora. Not to mention Evan —"

"I'm telling you," Carson insisted, "the best thing you can do is to stay away from him."

Hayley cleared her throat. "You're repeating yourself, Carson."

His voice was strained. "You're not answering me, Hayley."

She set her back against the drifting afternoon sun and turned to face him directly. "I wasn't aware you had asked a question."

He tried to conceal his frustration. "I'm serious, Hayley. Leave Newhaven."

Hayley dug at the chalky dirt under her nails. "No."

Carson blew out a long, low breath and stared at Hayley with an intensity that shook her to her core. For a moment, time seemed to stand still, and she found herself wishing that the next moment did not have to come...sensing that what came next would forever change all that had come before.

But time could not be manipulated by the will.

"All right then," Carson said in a voice so emotionless, he might have been asking Hayley how she liked her eggs cooked. "I wish you luck." The shadow fell back over Hayley as he moved to stand.

"Wh — what do you mean, you wish me luck?" Hayley felt her heart skip a beat. She rose beside Carson and searched his face.

"I mean, I hope things go well for you. But I won't be here to see it." He looked at her sadly, but she knew he was already pulling back and making an effort to control his feelings.

Hayley wanted to feign disinterest, but the question had to be asked. "Where are you going?"

"I'm not sure exactly." Carson sounded unconcerned. His expression was perfectly controlled. "Gabe and I have an aunt in Cornwall. We may start there." A hint of real feeling crept back into his voice, and he let himself meet Hayley's gaze. "I've simply got to get Gabe out of here. This isn't a safe place for him any more. I feel so much hatred toward the Harringtons, and Gabe is starting to feel it, too. He showed too much pleasure at seeing them fight. It isn't good. It's not how our mother would want him raised.

"Besides —" he faltered. "Now, I know you think I'm off, but I'm not convinced those two are harmless. I want to protect Gabe. I want to protect —" He stretched out a hand as if to touch Hayley's cheek but quickly let it fall. "I need to protect my family as best I can. At this point, I can't help but think that must mean taking Gabriel to a place where the Harringtons can no longer have an influence on him. A job is just a job." He didn't sound convinced. "Newhaven will just have to find another gardener. My family's involvement at the estate must come to an end."

"But —" Hayley protested. "What about Jenny?"

"I'll talk to our friends in town…have them watch for her. And I'll speak to Theadora. She and I don't exactly have a 'mutual admiration society' going," he admitted, "but I can't imagine her purposely keeping Jenny from her family. She always liked my sister, I think. Even though she wouldn't get involved, she seemed truly sorry when Jen disappeared. I'm fairly certain she'd do what she could to bring us back together."

"I see." Hayley could think of nothing else to say.

"You know," he tried one last time, "you'll leave too, if you're smart."

This should have set Hayley off, but she was consumed by her distress. "You may be right," she allowed. "But right now, I have to stay."

Carson nodded. "That's your decision," he said stiffly. "And I shall respect it." He took her grimy paw in his large, warm right hand. "I suppose this is it, then."

"I suppose it is," Hayley tried to answer cheerfully, but her voice cracked a bit on the last word.

The man before her cleared his throat and forced a half-hearted grin. "All right, then. It's been...wonderful working with you. You've quite a talent, you know." Hayley could not answer. "Yes...well." He blinked. "You're — uh — welcome." The furious blinking continued, and he went on brightly, "Well, good luck to you. I would say 'keep in touch,' but I can't imagine exactly how —" His voice broke. Emerald eyes glistened as he looked down upon her. "Good-bye, Hayley." His voice dropped to a whisper, and he tried to smile. "Don't forget me this time, hm?"

Hayley clutched at his hand as if it were hope. This wasn't what she wanted. But she couldn't stop him, could she? He was right; he and Gabe had to get on with their lives. But to lose him forever? She felt herself growing faint and offered up a silent prayer, asking God to keep her from falling flat. "Good-bye, Carson," she heard a husky voice utter. Everything inside her called to her to stop him. But he hadn't given any indication that he could be convinced to stay. Had he? "I promise...." Her voice shook. "I shall never forget you again."

Strong, slim fingers traced gently the curve of her jaw line. Then, with one last, watery smile, Carson leaned forward and placed a tender kiss upon her brow, then roughly turned away.

Hayley tried but was unable to watch him leave. Shaking hands buried themselves in the cool earth as silent tears dropped onto her pile of loam, and Hayley silently prayed to see, once more, God's hand in the cycle of life and death.

Twenty-One

I loved him not; and yet now he is gone/I feel I am alone.
Walter Savage Landor, *The Maid's Lament*

Round and round, Hayley stirred her stew as the aroma of oxtails and peppercorns mingled with the scent of neighboring lilacs. Bright carrot slices and golden fried onions bobbed invitingly in the savory broth, but she could not bring herself to eat. Nourishment was not a concern; she concentrated on sinking a chunk of turnip with her heavy spoon.

Twenty-four hours had passed since she and Carson had bid each other farewell. Since that time, and especially during that first day, Hayley had carefully kept herself occupied with various tasks around the grounds. It was easy to justify the labor. With both Carson and Gabriel leaving, she would need to shoulder an extra-large workload if the gardens weren't to suffer. Even Theadora was willing to accept greater responsibility, asserting that between her knowledge and Hayley's youth and energy there was nothing the two women could not accomplish on their own.

And so, while Carson and Gabriel had thrown themselves into packing up their modest belongings, Hayley had buried herself in fertilizer — both figuratively and literally — stopping her work just long enough to bid a tearful good-bye to the friendly boy who had stolen her heart. Then, as quickly as they had come into her life, both Elliotts were gone, leaving Hayley with a sense of longing that made her former loneliness seem like a mere mood swing.

She gave the skin of her soup a tiny slap with her spoon, sending broth and browned onions sloshing over the edge of her bowl and into her peas.

"Hullo, there!" exclaimed a friendly voice. "Didn't anyone ever teach you not to play with your food?"

Hayley looked up at the stylish man who regarded her with such amusement. "Oh, hello, Simon," she replied woodenly. "Sorry. Of course you're right." She lay the utensil down on the wrought-iron table with a clank.

"That's quite all right." Simon shrugged. "It's nothing to me. But what's this?" He leaned down and examined her sad face. "I hope you don't mind me saying, but…you look a bit rum. Is Theadora working you too hard?" His voice was thick with concern.

"No, no," Hayley waved the question aside. "I'm fine. *Really.*" She forced a smile in an attempt to set her companion's mind at ease. "Won't you sit down?"

"Don't mind if I do!" Iron grated against stone as Simon pulled a chair up beside her. The man looked characteristically cool in his pine-colored camp shirt and khaki shorts. In contrast, Hayley was sure she must appear hot and sticky in her cut-offs and a grimy, gray tee. But she couldn't drum up the energy to care. Appearances ranked somewhere just below nourishment on her list of priorities today. "I suppose you've had a hard time of it, with Elliott gone," Simon went on.

Hayley steeled herself for the Carson-bashing she knew would come, but he surprised her. "You know, it's really too bad," he admitted. "I know Elliott was difficult to get along with, but he did quite famously at his job. It will be a bit rough on you, now that he's gone." Simon sounded sincere in his expression of sympathy. "Although, I'm certain it's excellent training for you. I wouldn't be surprised if Theadora asked you to stay on after your time is done," he suggested hopefully, helping himself to the basket of rolls.

Hayley avoided his eyes. "I can't think that far ahead," she said quietly.

"Quite so." Simon scooted his iron chair an inch closer to Hayley's. He paused, seemingly thinking, then ventured, casually, "I suppose you've heard that Isabelle's gone back to London?"

Hayley did not answer. She *had* heard. But she hadn't cared. All her thoughts had centered around Carson...and Gabe. Why was it so difficult to let them go? *Is it because I feel responsible somehow? Could I have done something to make it possible for them to stay?*

"Like you said, I had to decide for myself whether or not things would work between Issy and me," Simon was telling her. "The more I thought about it, the clearer it became. She and I weren't right for each other. I know that now." He looked to Hayley for approval. "I want you to know that it was just as you said it should be. You needn't worry, Hayley. My decision was made independent of you."

Hayley tried to imagine how she should respond. Simon's relationship with Isabelle held little interest for her. But the man's face revealed such bare emotion, she could not help but relent. She gave her best attempt at a smile of agreement. "It's all right, Simon. I'm sure you did the best thing." It was clear from the beginning that the couple had trust issues. No other course of action save counseling, Hayley imagined, could have led to a satisfactory resolution.

"I did, didn't I?" Simon smiled gratefully. He reached out to pat her hand, but pulled back as he dragged one arm through the soupy mess on the table. Dark eyebrows met over the bridge of his nose as he regarded the spill, then examined her more closely. "And yourself?" he asked suspiciously. "How are you keeping?"

"How I'm *keeping*," Hayley sighed, "is busy." Simon continued to study her, but she turned her face away. Ever since she and Carson had spoken, she'd felt out of sorts. But how could she explain? She herself did not understand her feelings.

"You've a clock like a fiddle," Simon ventured sympathetically.

Hayley glanced up from her soup and wrinkled her nose. "I beg your pardon?"

"You know," he spoke with exaggerated seriousness. "Your face. *Long.*" He stretched out his features in a caricature of Hayley's glum expression.

She grinned despite herself. "All right. I get your point."

Pleased to have brightened her mood, Simon continued to mug for her, gnashing his teeth in mock fierceness and wiping from his eyes imaginary tears of grief.

"That's enough!" Hayley laughed and swatted him with her spoon. "I'm sure I don't look *that* bad!"

Her companion concluded his mocking with a smile of affection. "No, of course not," he agreed cheerfully. "In fact, you look smashing to me."

Hayley glanced at him out of the corner of one eye. He spoke casually enough. Was he making a pass? "Simon...." Her voice held warning.

"What?" The man opened his eyes wide, looking the picture of innocence. "I'm simply being matey! You know you have a bit of the sulks. Why don't you let me take you out?"

The last thing Hayley needed was a night of forced socializing. "Oh, I don't know...," she faltered.

"Well, I *do*," Simon spoke matter-of-factly, ignoring her protest. "You've been squirreled away ever since your arrival!" he proclaimed. "A night out will do you good. You like to dance, don't you?" He sounded as if every woman loved to dance. "Put on your best frock, and I'll show you the town!" He beamed in delight, obviously pleased with his suggestion. Hayley hesitated, but he was not deterred by her lack of enthusiasm. "Come on. Give over!" Simon urged. He looked at her closely, and his voice softened. "Look, I can see you've hit a dark patch. I hope we're not responsible?" He smiled the awkward half-smile of the guilty. "I suppose the row we put you through yesterday was a bit off-putting. I *am* sorry." He reached for her hand once more, this time ignoring the soup. "Do say you forgive me."

His plea touched Hayley's heart, and she began to relax. This was the one friend she had left at Newhaven. "Simon!" She laughed and squeezed his hand in return. *"You've* certainly nothing to feel sorry for. You're the one who stuck up for me. Oh!" Gratitude and memory hit her at the same time. "How's your poor nose?" She leaned across her bowl to get a better look, just as Simon bent forward to show off his wound; the two found themselves suddenly and unexpectedly with their faces mere millimeters apart.

At first, neither moved. Then Hayley shuddered involuntarily as Simon exhaled and his warm breath caressed her cheek. Feelings of fondness gave way to a more primitive emotion as she gazed into the eyes that held recognition of her pain and...something else Hayley could not name. During their conversation, she had sensed that Simon wanted to comfort her. Now it appeared as though he intended to kiss her, as well. She felt herself falling into the depths of his compassionate, gray-eyed gaze....

"No, Simon!" She pulled back abruptly. Simon blinked, like a former blind man getting his first glimpse of light. He appeared surprised, then frustrated. For a moment, he even looked irritated, but the expression was quickly replaced by one of entreaty.

"Hayley." His voice was thick with feeling. "Please. Don't pull away...."

"No." Hayley scooted back in her seat and kept her voice firm. "I'm serious, Simon. This isn't what I want."

He looked as though he did not want to believe her. "Is it because of the family ties?" he tried hopefully. "You realize, don't you, that it's a very distant connection.."

"It isn't the family." Hayley almost laughed. The situation was absurd. "Simon, this just isn't right. You and I...don't belong together. We never did, and we never will." She spoke gently. "I suspect you know that as well as I." Hayley held her breath. After all the Harrington theatrics she had witnessed, she half-expected Simon to throw a fit like Evan had when she'd rejected him. But the man seemed determined to accept her decision with dignity.

"All right, then," he conceded reluctantly. "I suppose that's that."

Hayley received his response with a sigh of relief. "Thank you for not pushing, Simon." The respect he showed her made him even more endearing than did his most polished pass.

"Although," he continued light-heartedly, "I can't imagine why you won't have me! It *must* have something to do with the family. I suppose you want nothing more than to escape as soon as possible. Isn't that so?"

"I...haven't really decided," Hayley admitted.

"Well, if I were in your place," Simon suggested in a low voice, "I'd be quite narked, after all that Theadora had done to you. *And* your parents." A look of pity filled his eyes. "I know about your father, Hayley. How bloody awful!"

"Well —" Hayley hated to deceive him. "It's not exactly an issue I want to pursue," she admitted hesitantly.

Simon eyed her with great curiosity. "What's this? Aunt T and Uncle David were responsible for your father's death, and you're saying you don't care a dash?"

"Oh, I care," Hayley assured him. "It's just that..." She glanced around furtively. It would not do for Theadora to know the truth just yet. "Well, actually...my father didn't really drown in the river."

"Cor!" Simon's eyes flew open wide, and he flashed her a delighted grin. "You don't say! Why, that means —" Suddenly his face grew pale. "That is, all this time..." he stuttered.

"I know! *Believe* me, I know," she told him.

"Well, then," Simon breathed. "You are the genuine heir to Newhaven, then. No question about it. Oh!" he clucked. "Poor Evan."

"What? I..." Hayley struggled to grasp his full meaning. "But I didn't intend to —"

"Of course not." The man spoke reassuringly, but he seemed slightly distracted. "And no one will imagine that you did."

Hayley was truly alarmed now. "Simon, please! You must make Evan understand. I don't mean to take his place. I just —"

"Now, there, there," Simon soothed her. He flashed her the familiar Harrington grin. "I'll go speak with him now, if you like. There's no reason to put it off."

"No!" Hayley protested. "I don't want anyone to know yet. I never should have —"

"There, there! Relax," Simon urged, patting her arm gently. "Don't worry. Of course I shan't say a word until you give me the sign." He did not appear to be concerned about Evan's loss. In fact, he almost seemed pleased. With a loud scraping noise, he pushed his iron chair back and appeared ready to stand.

"Simon…," Hayley warned.

"Now, now! I promised to hold my tongue, and I shall," he told her cheerfully. "For now. I'll tell him when you think the time is right. But don't worry about old Evan. It will be good for him. And I'm sure he'll take it in stride."

Hayley smiled at him gratefully. "I'm a coward to let you do my dirty work," she said, feeling foolish. "But that won't keep me from accepting your help." She followed him with her eyes as he stood.

"Finish your stew, now," he ordered, as if directing a small child, then reached forward and tucked a stray tendril of hair behind Hayley's ear.

"Thank you, Simon," she whispered gratefully, then watched his retreat.

She was still staring at the open doorway several minutes after he'd gone. What was wrong with her? She liked Simon. He was kind, gentle, devoted...and obviously smitten with her. After all she'd been through — was still going through — it should have been the easiest, most natural response in the world to fall into his arms and accept his comfort.

But as Hayley tried to picture herself wrapped in his comforting embrace, her mind refused to conjure up the solid, athletic frame that belonged to Simon Harrington. Instead, time and time again she imagined herself enveloped in the long, lean limbs of a quirky man whose grasshopper-like form was now nothing more than a memory.

Round and round, she stirred the stew. The aroma was gone. Even the scent of lilac had ceased to linger. It seemed only fitting. For as Hayley reflected on all she'd lost, it seemed that life itself had lost its flavor.

Twenty-Two

❧

And all alone went she.
Charles Kingsley, *The Sands of Dee*

Hayley nodded her approval as the Peugeot slipped uncomplainingly into third gear. She nearly ventured a smile. Perhaps the day-trip would be fairly painless after all.

After her disastrous encounter with the Mini, Hayley was less than enthusiastic at the prospect of suffering through another adventure on Britain's motorways. But Ellen's words had left her little choice in the matter.

"Well, now, Reverend Archer would be the one to ask," the maid answered in response to Hayley's questioning. "And as I said, he's in London for a day or two, visiting his sister." She scratched her small, white brow. "I do recall something about a slow man, down in Widow's Glen, who goes by that name. Surely he cannot be the one you mean? What would you be needing with such a man?"

Hayley quickly assured Ellen that he most certainly wasn't the man she was looking for, then immediately proceeded to request the woman's aid in procuring her a car. An hour later, her battle-scarred travel map and precious yellow envelope tucked securely in her handbag, Hayley gratefully accepted the keys to Theadora's sleek black auto and scurried out the front door, her regular work clothes discarded in favor of a white cotton lawn shirt and classic tan capri pants. In answer to Ellen's questioning gaze, she had mumbled something unconvincing about driving into Harrington's Green for postcards and scurried out the front door.

Hayley pressed the pedal for more gas, and the auto responded reassuringly. During her trip from London through the Chilterns, Hayley had driven her Mini at an embarrassingly slow speed, yet other travelers had seemed unconcerned and had managed to pass her easily. Today, she noticed an increase in traffic that played upon her nerves. Particularly annoying was the gray car in her mirror that refused to pass at any speed. However, Hayley had managed to carefully wind her way back up the gently sloping hills to the designated cut-off. Only the final crossroads eluded her. Once she got used to the other cars on the road, Hayley realized that the journey would not be a difficult one. By her estimate, Widow's Glen was less than three kilometers from the Green: the residents could practically be considered neighbors, if one cared to make the effort to visit.

Unfortunately, "visiting" was not what her journey was about. In her mind's eye, Hayley read and re-read the words that had sent her on her ridiculous mission:

...I do not know if you will return to the chapel before this evening. I will proceed as we have planned, unless given the word to do otherwise by Galen or the reverend.

Initially, Hayley had intended to talk with Reverend Archer;

in his absence, she hoped that the mysterious Galen might shed some light on her father's reputed "death." Without a last name, she had little to go on; Ellen's description of a "slow" man discouraged her even further. Yet any course of action, no matter how absurd, was better than none at all.

A signpost up ahead alerted Hayley to the cut-off for Widow's Glen. Her fingers tingling with sweat and anticipation, she gripped the steering wheel tightly and maneuvered the Peugeot down the hill toward a group of lovingly restored brick and timber cottages almost identical to those in Harrington's Green.

Buoyed by the sight and encouraged by her successful journey, Hayley parked the auto almost like an expert, then strolled into the largest building in sight: a beautiful white stone affair emblazoned with the words Crown Royal Hotel.

Inside, Hayley was met by an eager, teen-aged bellboy with bright eyes and oversized ears.

"May I help you, miss?" the young man asked with an awkward half-bow.

"I hope so." Turning on the charm, Hayley flashed a brilliant smile. "You see, I'm looking for someone who lives in this town, and I've *no* idea where to begin."

Staring at her with obvious admiration, the young man fell right into her trap. "I say...I've lived here for quite some time. I dare say I can help you," he offered, puffing out his chest.

"Oh, that would be *wonderful!*" Hayley exclaimed. "It's not a terribly common name, I gather. I'm looking for a man named 'Galen.' I suppose he'd be, oh...at least thirty years of age, although he could be quite a bit older."

"Well...." The helpful smile fell from the boy's face. "We've a man here named Galen, but..." he faltered. "Do you mind if I ask —? That is, we're a bit protective of Galen around here. And I —"

"Of course!" Hayley assured him warmly. "You want to know whether I would be disturbing him...and I promise you I would not. Galen knew my father years ago, and I just wanted to —" She hesitated for a split-second while she searched for the right words. "Well, I guess you could say *reminisce* about the old days." *Perfect. Not even close to an untruth.*

"We-ell. It sounds all right..." The boy seemed to be considering.

Hayley's gentle lips curved up at either side, revealing brilliant, white teeth. "If you like, you can come along and listen for yourself," she offered, knowing full well the young man could not leave his post.

"I'm afraid I can't do that," he said, sounding genuinely remorseful. "But —" Hayley's willingness seemed to sway him. "It doesn't sound as though you mean him any harm. I could tell you which cottage is his family's. He's nearly always to be found at home."

"You're *very* kind," she gushed. Inspired by her appreciation, the young man pulled out a tourist flyer and scribbled out a rough map for Hayley.

"It's the fourth one on the right, after you turn the corner. If you reach the pub, you've gone too far," he cautioned.

She thanked him profusely and headed back onto the street. To her left lay a bustling, open marketplace, but Hayley kept her sights on the map in her hand and the mission on her heart. "Pass one, two...three cottages on the right, then turn west..." She stopped as a familiar feeling caused the hairs on the nape of her neck to rise. The bellboy? Hayley turned abruptly, but the young man was nowhere in sight. Still, she could not shake the feeling that she was being followed. Hayley scanned the crowd but could find no evidence that she was being watched.

Her heart filled with a sense of foreboding. It was bad enough to be trailed back at Newhaven. But if someone were stalking her now, who could she turn to for help? She weighed her options: Head back to the manor or finish her task. Glancing furtively over her shoulder one last time, Hayley decided to take the risk. She was probably imagining things. Besides, what kind of idiot would attack her in the main square?

Filled with resolve, but with her confidence shaken, Hayley concentrated on the flyer in her hand. Obeying the directions carefully, she turned right at the next corner and followed the cobblestone path.

Focusing on the challenge ahead, she tried to imagine what she could say to this man when she actually found him. *"Hi. You don't know me, but I read your name in a note my mother wrote to my father twenty-six years ago and thought you might be involved in the cover-up of his death? Actually, I don't know if it was your name at all, but I thought I'd accuse you anyway…"* The prospect gave her reason to pause and reflect. It was because she did so that she heard the footsteps.

From all around she could hear the sound of heels clicking against stone. But somehow, Hayley knew instinctively that the steps behind her were different. It may have been the urgent pace, or the alarming proximity of her pursuer. Perhaps it was the unusual stride…

A hard, sinewy hand gripped her shoulder and spun her

around before she could cry out. Hayley opened her mouth to protest, but the scream died in her throat as she found herself gazing into the soulful eyes of the only man she had ever loved.

"Carson!" The word fell from her lips like an endearment.

"You remembered." His smile touched the depths of her soul.

"But, what —" She caught her breath and lay one hand against his faded, old polo, as if to reassure herself that he was real. "Where did you…?"

"We turned back at Bath," Carson explained, his voice thick with emotion. "I was worried about you. I've been following you since the main road." His gaze was searching. "Did you really think I could leave you?"

"I…" Hayley gazed at him with wide, dark eyes. Her voice would not come.

His keen eyes flickered across her face, taking in the blush of her cheeks, the slope of her nose…the fullness of her sweet, gentle lips. With arms that shook, he drew her into a fierce embrace and muttered against the softness of her hair, "How could *I* imagine myself capable of such a thing?" He held her tight for several long moments, then released her so that he could gaze into her face once more. "Hayley," he began raggedly, his hands gently gripping her upper arms, "I've known for weeks how I feel, but I didn't know if I should say…" His voice broke off. He tried again, "I should have done, but I —" He looked as if he might give in to the temptation to speak without words, but then he made one final, valiant effort, "Hayley Buckman, you are the most incredible person I have ever met in my life." His eyes sparkled with the hint of tears. "I am in awe of the woman that you are.

"I admire your wit, your laughter…your determination and your gentle spirit. I love the way you've reached out to Gabriel." Carson let out a hearty laugh. "The boy adores you." He sobered and spoke in a low voice. "But not half as much as I do. Hayley, I love you." A look of uncertainty crossed his features. "I had to tell you. I don't know how you feel, but —"

Tears of happiness welled up in Hayley's eyes, and she threw herself back into Carson's arms. "You love me? But how?" she mumbled against the softness of his shirt. "Gabriel said you were smitten with Francine."

Carson threw back his head and let out a delighted roar. "Oh, *that!* I asked Gabe about that conversation the last time you mentioned it. All he told you, my dear, was that I was smitten. He didn't say a thing about *who* —"

Hayley drew in a sharp breath and pulled her head back to fix him with her gaze. "You're joking! Surely he didn't mean *me?*"

Carson grinned like an idiot. "Why not?"

"Well, for heaven's sake," she protested. "I had just arrived!"

"Exactly!" Carson looked pleased. "Hence the word 'smitten.'" He raised one eyebrow expressively. "It wasn't until later that I even thought the word 'love.'"

"Oh, really?" Hayley smiled and burrowed deeper into his embrace. "How *much* later?"

Carson tightened his arms around her. "To my surprise — and dismay I might add —" he said jokingly, "not much later at all. I was already quite taken by the time you told me my flowers had dropped a brick."

"Hey!" Hayley pounded on his chest with one tiny fist. "I thought we covered this already! I told you I thought you meant that you had left the note —"

"Yes…yes…yes. So you say *now* —" Carson rolled his eyes.

"Hmm," Hayley mumbled comfortably, not threatened by his joking. "And what do you mean by it being to your 'dismay'?"

Carson grew serious. "Well, I admit, I would never have chosen to fall in love this deeply, this fast." He wrapped a tendril of Hayley's thick hair around his index finger and smiled at her gently. "But I promise you, I don't regret the feeling." She looked up at him, her face filled with delight. "That is…" He hesitated uncertainly. "At least I don't so far! But then, you haven't really told me how you feel…"

Hayley placed her two warm hands on either side of Carson's angular face and told him, breathlessly, "Carson Elliott, you wonderful, incredible man! Just when I thought I'd lost everything, God gave me a new family, the beginnings of hope…and now an unbelievable new love! I *do* love you. I love you with all of my heart, spirit, and soul." As his lips lowered upon hers, she had just enough time to whisper with feeling, "And don't you forget it!"

Twenty-Three

Something hidden. Go and find it....
Lost and waiting for you. Go.
Rudyard Kipling, *The Explorer*

It was several long minutes before Hayley and Carson realized that they had become the focus of not a few stares from curious locals. Grinning shamelessly, they tore themselves with great reluctance from each other's arms and proceeded to walk together, hand-in-hand, in the pale English sun, while smiling idiotically like a pair of bashful teenagers.

Hayley wound her fingers tightly between Carson's. "So that was you following me?" she realized incredulously, remembering the auto that would not pass.

"Mm-hmm," Carson admitted, his attention focused on her graceful profile.

"I wondered what that car's problem was," she mumbled, pretending to have been genuinely disturbed. "Why didn't you just honk and let me know it was you?"

"I wasn't sure whether you wanted to see me again," Carson admitted, relief at Hayley's welcome clearly written all over his face. "I thought perhaps you'd be angry. I wasn't sure I even dared to show myself. At first, I thought I might just follow you at a distance…keep an eye on you, in case you should fall into any trouble."

"Yeah, well…some private eye *you* are," Hayley accused, screwing up her face in an unsuccessful attempt at a look of disapproval. "I knew I was being followed. I sensed it."

Carson laughed at her ridiculous expression. "I saw you looking around. I could tell you had got the jim jams."

Hayley sniffed defensively. "Well, I had!"

"I know," the gardener admitted, giving her fingers a sympathetic squeeze. "That's why I decided to show myself. I could tell I had frightened you, and I wanted you to feel safe."

"Mmm," Hayley drew his arm around her and snuggled up under the warm curve of his shoulder. "It worked."

"All right, then." Carson smiled at her protectively. "I suppose the only question left is: What on earth are we doing in Widow's Glen?"

"What?" Hayley stared up at him in surprise. It suddenly struck her that he was unaware of her plan to root out the cause of her father's death rumor. Quickly, she brought him up to date as they advanced upon the cottage in question.

"Would you like to be the one to try?" Hayley offered hopefully.

"No, no," Carson demurred but continued to hold her. "This is your mission. I shan't intrude."

"Really, it's all right," she tried to assure him, but they had already reached the front step. "Oh, fine!" she grumbled, squeezing his hand fiercely. Carson obviously realized she was nervous, yet he was encouraging *her* to be the one to follow through. After all she had gone through, it would have been the easiest thing in the world to let him handle the situation. But in her heart, she was glad he had not tried to step in and rescue her. Although she cherished his support, she also greatly desired to build and maintain her own inner strength. Clinging to this thought, she smiled boldly and tackled head-on the task before her. "Here goes nothing!" Sounding more courageous than she felt, Hayley tapped out a cheerful beat on the heavy wooden door.

A shuffling sound came from within, and the door was quickly opened by the owner of a wide, toothy grin. The man stood half a head taller than the gentleman on his steps, but he could have matched two of Carson in thickness. Bloodshot eyes darted from one guest to the other, and the man's thick lips stretched back over yellowed teeth in a grimace of delight.

"I say!" the toothy one exclaimed happily. "Visitors!"

Hayley returned the smile with her own friendly gaze. "Hello!" she said politely. "My name is Hayley Buckman — I'm visiting from the States. And this is Carson Elliott. I hate to disturb you, but we're looking for a man named Galen."

The man nodded enthusiastically. "Visitors!" he repeated. Unfortunately, he was apparently unaccustomed to greeting company, for once he had identified Hayley and Carson as such, he could do nothing but stare and seemed at a loss to know what to do with the two precious guests now that he had them.

"May we come in?" Hayley suggested finally. This request triggered a response; the man stepped away from the door and led them to a saggy golden sofa before slipping once more into staring mode.

"Are you Galen, then?" Hayley questioned him. The man beamed and nodded again. Although he seemed to nod at everything, Hayley decided to take the action as genuine affirmation. "Well, as I said before, I'm Hayley," she told him in a friendly tone. "You and I have not met before, but my father once knew a man named Galen. I was hoping you might be that man," Hayley explained carefully. She tried to guess at the year of Galen's birth, but the openness of his expression gave him the appearance of a giant child. The man seemed ageless.

"Did you ever meet a man named Jonathan Buckman, Galen?" Hayley tried. But before she had even begun, she realized she had lost the battle. Already, the man had forgotten his visitors; his attention was re-focused on the model ship he was building.

He wandered over to the kitchen table and the pile of sticks that occupied his most pressing thoughts. "What about your home, Galen?" Hayley went on firmly. "Did *you* ever live in Harrington's Green? Do you have friends there?" Hayley posed the questions again and again, varying the sentence structure and tone slightly each time. She quickly discovered that if she put her face quite close to Galen's, he would turn and offer her a happy grin. Otherwise, he simply concentrated on his sticks and glue.

Her discouragement mounting, Hayley finally tried one last appeal. "Galen, where's your family?" She glanced about the room for clues. *"What about your family?"* She spoke with a voice that was slow and clear.

"They must work during the day," Carson suggested. "He seems accustomed to caring for himself."

Hayley nodded and turned away from her subject, but the

question had already triggered a response in Galen. "I have family in Harrington's Green," he announced matter-of-factly. "Uncle Rupert, Rupert. I *like* Uncle Rupert." A wooden stick fell to the ground and rolled under the table; Galen hopped down onto the floor to retrieve it.

Hayley let him go. She stared at Carson in wonder. "Reverend Archer?" Her voice was little more than a whisper. They had the right man. *This* was the Galen of her mother's note. She turned back to their simple host, who was crawling about beneath the table. "What *about* Uncle Rupert, Galen?" Hayley plopped down on her hands and knees to help him in his search. "Did you ever go stay with Uncle Rupert?" she asked as she rescued the stick from its position under an oily caster. "Do you remember Uncle Rupert's friend Jonathan?" She and Carson each took one arm and helped the man to his knees.

Galen's head bobbed up and down as he dove back into his pile of sticks. "Uncle Rupert. Uncle Rupert." Just saying the words seemed to bring him joy. Nothing else seemed to reach him, although Hayley spent nearly twenty minutes trying. After giving it her best effort, Hayley realized that her line of questioning was getting them nowhere.

"Oh, Carson!" She wanted to cry in frustration. "This isn't helping a bit!"

"I know," the man admitted. "Look, why don't we just head back into town? Any information you might have gotten from Galen you can get from Reverend Archer himself when he returns."

"I know. You're right." Trying to hide her disappointment, Hayley smiled kindly at their host and handed him his offending piece of boat. It wasn't Galen's fault that he couldn't understand or didn't remember; she reached over and patted the man on his thick shoulder as she stood.

"Besides, it was a long time ago," Carson reasoned, moving to join her. "He probably wouldn't have remembered Jon no matter what we said." He took Hayley by the hand, and the two moved as if to let themselves out the front door. In doing so, they almost missed the change that had occurred in Galen when Carson mentioned the shortened version of Jonathan's name.

"Big Jon. Big Jon," Galen mumbled to himself, then got increasingly louder. "Big Jon heavy. Oh, so heavy! Big Jon is gone, but oh, how heavy!"

"He remembers!" Hayley exclaimed and turned back into the room. But try as they might, all they could get from Galen was, "Big Jon. *Heavy* Jon." In the end, there was nothing left to do but thank him and see themselves out.

"He lives in his own little world," Hayley concluded sadly after the door had closed behind them. "I don't think he remembered a thing."

"I'm sorry," Carson sympathized, squeezing her shoulders with one lanky arm. They walked back toward their cars in silence. "You know, it's funny," Carson ventured, "all he said about your father being so big. You're just a bit of a thing," he observed. "I didn't remember Jon being quite so big as to have made such an impression on Galen."

"But he wasn't really," Hayley protested. "That's what makes me think Galen doesn't really remember."

"He wasn't a terribly tall man?" Carson wondered out loud. "Not overweight…or overly muscular?"

"No." Hayley shook her head in bewilderment. "Not a bit. He was just your average guy, really."

"Hunh," Carson grunted thoughtfully. "That's odd. I can't imagine what would make Galen remember him like that. Maybe it was some private joke that started before Jon's death. Like calling a big guy 'Tiny,' or like —"

"*Carson!*" Hayley clutched at his arm and drew in a sharp breath.

"What?" He stopped by the Peugeot and looked at her in alarm.

"But that's it. *That's it!*" Her face lit up in understanding. "*That's* why Evan has been following me…why he tried to woo me. He figured I knew something the rest of the family didn't. And he was right! I know my father wasn't buried at Newhaven in 1969." For Hayley, fact and reason met at last on the warm English countryside. "But something else *was*. Something big. Something heavy."

Carson's jaw fell in as he followed her train of thought. "You think…the Nollekens statue?"

Hayley nodded, full realization beginning to dawn on her. "That's right. 'Big Jon's' death caused a lot trouble…" She smiled in satisfaction at the thought, then sobered as she realized the meaning of her discovery.

"And now, someone's looking for a *big* pay-off."

Twenty-Four

❧

*It is sufficiently agreed that all things change, and
that nothing really disappears....*
Francis Bacon, *Cogitationes de Natura Rerum*

It makes perfect sense!" Hayley used her slim, tanned fingers to tick off points as she made her case. "We know Reverend Archer was in on my father's disappearance. We know there was a small memorial service at the grave site, with only my mother and your parents in attendance. But someone had to have helped the reverend bury the casket beforehand." Her dark eyes danced as the scenario unfolded in her mind. "Who better to help him than someone whose personal challenges would keep him from noticing that anything was wrong? Okay," she admitted, "so Galen kept mentioning that Jon was 'heavy.' But who on earth would take that to mean the box carried far more weight than that of an ordinary man?"

"Not a soul," Carson agreed as he navigated the Peugeot around a difficult corner. Back in Widow's Glen, the Renault awaited its retrieval, having been abandoned by the couple in their eagerness to get back to Newhaven and the treasure waiting there. "The question then is, why would Reverend Archer burglarize a valuable statue? I've known the man my entire life." He shook his head in disbelief. "It's simply not in character for him to steal."

"I don't think he saw it as stealing," Hayley considered thoughtfully, remembering Simon's description of the statue's disappearance: *"Of course, Reverend Archer was thrilled. He always thought the thing was sinful. He took very seriously the fact that it was an image of a pagan god."* "I gather he was quite disturbed by the piece. He may have thought he was doing his parish a favor, what with the church and gardens being connected and all."

"I can see that of him," her companion admitted. "He's a good man, but a bit obsessive. He tends to want to control people…sort of orchestrate their spiritual lives for them." Although he sounded disappointed, Carson seemed determined not to let the revelation bother him. "He means no harm. He just doesn't know how to let go and leave control to God."

Hayley twisted the corner of her lawn shirt between trembling hands, her anger starting to rise. "Well, that's all very well and good for him," she said hotly. "But what about my father? He's the one who took the blame for this little heist! My parents spent their entire lives cut off from their home and family, just because one man felt threatened by a piece of art!" One by one, tidbits of information fell into place for her. "Once the theft occurred, I'll bet David Harrington just seized the opportunity to get rid of my father. He probably couldn't have cared less about who really stole it. And Reverend Archer was more concerned about his own agenda than he was about my father's welfare!"

Her old feelings of disillusionment began to resurface. "You see, *this* is what I hate about organized religion. People act like their actions don't impact others. Everyone thinks he has a private line to God and anything that happens can be explained away as God's will! Even their own selfish choices." Carson listened without interrupting as long pent-up emotions spilled from Hayley's lips.

"This is *exactly* why I quit going to church," she continued unhappily. "Everyone focuses on the negatives of religion. 'Don't do this. You can't do that. Don't look at art. Don't listen to music with a beat.' I thought a relationship with God was supposed to be freeing, not isolating!" She slumped miserably against the car door, consumed by the feelings of frustration and confusion she'd hoped to have left behind after her experience at Newhaven chapel.

"Hunh. Talk about focusing on the negatives of religion!" Carson remarked dryly.

Hayley fixed him with a level glare. "Obviously you don't agree," she said coolly. "All right, spill it. What, exactly, are you trying to say?"

Carson shrugged casually. "Just that you seem to be guilty of the same crime that has offended you." Hayley dropped her eyes and looked away. "Hey!" The man's voice softened, and he tried to catch her gaze. "Look, I'm not disagreeing with you. I don't for a minute think Archer was justified in his actions. But we've all known Christians like him who have taken morality or faith into their own hands, but it doesn't *change* who God is.

"I'm not trying to discount the suffering you've felt," he assured her. "I think it's good and natural to examine our weaknesses and see where we, as a church, can do better. But this situation is *not* one that is unusual or unique to your life circumstances, Hayley.

"Even God acknowledges the problem in the Bible when he says to the Israelites, 'For the name of God is blasphemed among the Gentiles because of you.' How do you think that made him feel? He's God, for pity's sake, and his chosen people are running around, giving him a bad name." Hayley began to relax as she listened to the steady rhythm of his words.

"It isn't up to you, Hayley, to pass judgment or to hold a grudge," Carson went on gently. "People do the best they can — usually. Sometimes they act out of selfish motives. Sometimes they just make poor choices. But *they* alone are responsible for their actions. God is merciful, and God is just. He will deal with them. Your job is simply to focus on who God is. Love him...and let the rest go." Hayley felt a glimmer of peace return to her heart as the truth of his words sank in.

"Forgive your parents," Carson quietly urged. "Forgive the reverend...whatever his motives."

Hayley met his gaze. "And forgive the Harringtons?" she said simply.

Carson caught her meaning immediately. His eyes flickered back to the road. "Quite so," he acknowledged, smiling self-consciously. "I suppose now you'll tell me I should follow my own advice?"

"Well, now...that's up to you," Hayley flashed him a look of innocence. "Far be it from me to orchestrate your spiritual life for you..."

Hayley and Carson trudged through the garden, lugging the full arsenal of tools with which they were equipped to do battle with the earth. Dirt-covered shovels clanged against crusty-looking hoes, playing a cheerful accompaniment tune to their march.

Perspiration trickled down Hayley's face, and her shirt clung, damp against her small body. As they neared the grave-yard, her arms shook with the strain and excitement. She felt like a child in an adventure tale filled with pirates and treasure, and her heart leapt as she pictured Carson and herself digging up their "booty."

Even more thrilling was the satisfaction she felt in knowing she'd soon have the proof that was needed to absolve her father of any blame in the statue's disappearance. She marched confidently toward the marker that bore Jon Buckman's name. Her senses tingled in anticipation. So clear was her vision of the excavated grave, she could almost see the mounds of earth piled high before her eyes...

"Hullo, what's this?" Carson wondered aloud, then stopped abruptly, realization hitting him a split-second before it struck Hayley. "Blimey!"

Hayley suddenly felt weak. She relaxed her grip on the garden implements, and they fell to the ground in a deafening echo of her crashed hopes. Her unbelieving eyes scanned the ground before them. The memorial stone remained, but the evidence of Jon Buckman's innocence was gone.

"What?" Hayley could barely breathe. She began to sway. "How?"

Carson steadied her with a strong hand at her waist. "Apparently, we weren't the first ones to solve the mystery," he said grimly.

"But I don't understand!" Hayley pressed her hands against

her burning face. "How could anyone else —" A wave of nausea rushed over her as she recognized the awful truth. "Oh, no." A lump of hurt and anger rose in her throat. *"Simon."*

Carson did not ask if Hayley had revealed her secret; he did not have to.

Tears of betrayal burned in her eyes. "But I really thought he was different than Evan! I thought he was my *friend.* Oh, Carson! You tried to warn me…"

Carson's eyes revealed nothing but tender compassion. Not a hint of "I told you so" lurked in their depths.

"And there's nothing we can do to stop them!" Hayley wailed. "We can't turn Evan and Simon in to the police. We have no proof! Just a theory…and an empty hole." The injustice of the situation seemed almost unbearable. "Meanwhile, they'll go sell the statue on the black market. A *Nollekens.* My word! Who knows how much they'll get for it? They'll be set for life!"

Indignation regarding their illicit riches gave way to feelings of a much more personal nature. "And to think that all along, they were playing with me!" The more she thought about it, the more Hayley imagined she might really be sick. "First, Evan trying to win my affections, then his brother! All along, Simon kept trying to get me to *trust* him. He didn't love me! He just wanted me to let on about what I knew!" Scene after scene from the previous week played itself out in her mind. "What an idiot I was!" she chastised herself. "How could I think that they were sincere? That *both* of them would fall in love with me like that?"

"You could think it," Carson interrupted, "because there's nothing more believable." Taking her chin firmly in hand, he tilted Hayley's head upward and bathed her face in the warmth of his smile. "I don't know anyone, Hayley Buckman, who could be more likely to stir feelings of love in a man's heart."

Hayley felt her face flush hot with pleasure, but the emotion was fleeting. "Carson!" The pupils of her dark eyes were wide; she almost appeared to be in shock. "They tried so hard to turn me against you! Everything they said, all their warnings, and then that ridiculous fight..." Hayley shuddered in horror at the deviousness of their minds. Certainly, the whole thing was staged. Even Isabelle must have been in on it from the first. Hayley clutched at Carson's sleeve for a bit of tangible comfort. "What if they had succeeded? What if I had gone away?" She caught her breath. "What if you had never come back?"

Carson reached forward and tenderly smoothed a lock of Hayley's damp hair back into place. "Don't worry, poppet," he assured her, his eyes kind. "We said we'd trust God, didn't we?" He spoke the words with confidence, but as he enfolded her in his arms, he sighed raggedly, as if the prospect had shaken him, too, to his core. "God brought us together once. No... *Twice!*" he reminded her, smiling above her soft, sweet-smelling hair. "I knew he could do it again."

Together they stood, bound by love and sorrow, as the weak English sun sank low on the horizon. It was there that Gabriel found them, many minutes later, still whispering to one another words of tenderness and comfort.

"I say!" Gabe exclaimed as he approached. "I see Carson found you, Hayley." He eyed her curiously. "What did the wretched fellow say? You're all soppy."

Hayley detangled herself partially from Carson's embrace and threw her free arm around the young boy's shoulders. "The wretched fellow didn't say a single word that I'd let him take back. He's been an absolute dear."

"Quite right," Carson agreed, trying unsuccessfully to appear wounded by Gabriel's words. "I've been a *dear*. I'm surprised at you, lad, for suggesting otherwise."

"Hmph." Gabe shrugged, looking unconcerned. "Well, whatever he's said, Hayley, I hope he's managed to convince you to stay on at Newhaven?" he suggested hopefully.

Brown eyes twinkled as Hayley smiled up at the man who still held her firmly with one arm. "Hmm. Yes. Well, he's come up with some *fairly* convincing arguments..." She laughed as Carson's arm tightened fiercely at her waist.

"Hey! *Fairly* convincing?" he grumbled.

Hayley winked at Gabe. "I'll give it some thought," she promised solemnly.

"That's good," Gabriel gave a sigh of relief. "You know, nearly everyone has been trying to leave. First, Jenny. Next, Francine. Then Carson tried to take me away," he complained. "It's getting terribly difficult to get people to stay. Take old Evan and Simon, for instance..."

Startled, Carson dropped his arm from Hayley's shoulders. The color drained from the young woman's face, and she stared at Gabe, horrified. "You don't mean you actually *saw* them —"

"Oh, quote!" Gabriel assured her cheerfully. "The poor blokes were packing something enormous into a chartered trailer truck. Apparently, they planned to go on a long journey." He shook his head disapprovingly. "Of course, I knew they would regret it. I felt partially responsible, you know, because we've all had such a hard time of it lately. I felt sorry, so I decided to fix things." He waved one skinny hand, as if fending off their praise. "I know you think that was awfully decent of me. But I couldn't help but think that it's a bit of a do if neighbours can't help each other.

"And so," he prattled on, "I crawled right under the lorry and poked a bit of a hole in their fuel line. I figured that by the time they had found the problem and fixed it, they would realize their mistake and be ready to come home. I imagine they should run out of petrol perhaps halfway between here and London." He grinned with amusement at the bare shock on their faces.

"What's this? Oh, you're probably concerned about those chaps getting stuck on the motorway with that large, expensive package of theirs, and no way to get it home? Not to worry. I called ahead and alerted the constable. The constable should be meeting up with the old boys any time now —"

Any further explanation was cut short as Carson began to whoop and pound delightedly on Gabriel's back. "Pure dead brilliant! *Well done,* Gabriel!"

For Hayley, all feelings of fear and frustration fell away as Carson's words came back to her: *"God is merciful, and God is just....Love him...and let the rest go."* The God who had touched her heart in the chapel was in control. All would be well. He was there when she saw him; he was there when she did not. For the moment, she could only be thankful for the reminder of his sovereignty.

Hayley's eyes flickered from one shaggy-headed Elliott to the other. She could not settle in her mind which appeared more delighted: the devoted older brother, overflowing with familial pride, or the extraordinary young man who had brought joy into the life of the father figure he adored. "You've got them on a plate now, old boy!" Carson continued to thump furiously upon Gabriel's shoulders. "Good show!"

As she read the joy on the faces of the two most important men in her life Hayley felt her own heart brim, almost to overflowing, with the waters of emotion. To a spirit scarred by loss, the risk that lay ahead seemed almost unbearably great. But to a soul that had finally begun to heal, her tomorrows fairly gleamed with opportunity and hope.

Slowly, timidly at first, Hayley took a step toward her future.

And grinning the idiotic grins of delighted madmen, her future reached out and welcomed her with open arms.

$\mathscr{Epilogue}$

❧

Nunc scio quid sit Amor. Now I know what Love is.
Virgil, *Eclogue*

A sweet, delicate bouquet of fragrance rose from the bundle in Hayley's arms, tickling her nose and teasing her lips into a tender smile. During her long weeks at Newhaven, Hayley had been delighted by the bright, shining faces which adorned the vast gardens. But none had so captured her heart, none had so delighted her soul, as the child she loved as if she were Hayley's own.

The bundle squirmed. Instinctively, Hayley tightened her hold and lowered her head. "Are you all right, punkin?" she whispered against sweet, warm skin. But the tiny eyes remained closed against the sun. Soft, petal-like lips curved gently outward, reminding Hayley of a fresh blossom, just starting to bloom. She brushed her own mouth against the tiny, round cheeks and forehead, leaving a trail of feathery kisses from chin to brow.

The sound of leaves crackling underfoot caught Hayley's attention, and a movement across the garden caused her smile to transform into a full-fledged grin. Bidding the newcomer welcome with just her eyes, Hayley kept both arms wrapped around the precious bundle and watched the figure approach.

The young woman moved with the kind of quiet assurance that brought a thrill of pleasure to Hayley's heart. Just three months earlier, she had shown up looking tired and worn…and ashamed. Today, her tousled yellow curls bounced and twisted as she walked, and once-dull eyes now shone a bright, luminous green.

The blonde stepped to Hayley's side, then settled beside her upon one of the graceful garden swings Carson had recently added to accommodate the growing crowds. "Ah, Hayley. How's my Rosie?" Her high, young voice lowered in pitch on the last sentence, and she spoke with obvious pride.

"She's been an absolute angel." Hayley studied the woman with compassionate eyes. "Did you have a nice time today?"

"Hmmm." The blonde nodded her affirmation, but kept her attention focused on the child. Long, pale fingers fussed with the rose-colored quilt Hayley had drawn up over the baby's head, like a hood, to block the few pale beams of sunlight that shone through the giant yews. "It was smashing to get out for a bit, even just for tea. Thanks ever so much."

Keeping one hand tucked securely under the child, Hayley reached over with the other and squeezed her companion's arm. "It's good to have you home, Jenny."

The blonde smiled shyly in response. "It's good to *be* home. I hadn't realized how much I missed it!" She sighed. "That is, I knew I missed Carson and Gabe. I should have come home months ago," she admitted sadly. "I just felt that I had let everyone down. Especially Carson —"

"I know. I know, Jen." Hayley's voice was filled with compassion. She'd discussed the situation numerous times: not only with Jenny, but with Carson. Yet she knew that talking it through — as many times as necessary — was part of Jenny's healing process.

"He was good about it, though, wasn't he?" Jenny still sounded incredulous. "If it were me, I'd have been furious."

"Well, what can I say? Your brother is *incredible*. I can't say I've ever met anyone even remotely like him. You're terribly lucky to have him." Hayley's eyes glistened with the slightest hint of tears. "We *both* are," she whispered huskily.

Jenny's face was graced by a look of tenderness as Hayley's bundle let out a tiny wail. "Oh, Rosie!" Jenny clucked and reached for the baby. "Are you wet, sweetheart?" she wondered aloud, then after a quick examination proclaimed, "She's clean!" She rocked the child gently. "But I suspect she's probably hungry. I should — Hullo! What's this?" Jenny laughed as Rose dropped back asleep in her arms. "Blimey! Just when I think I've got this child figured out —"

Hayley set her feet against the ground beneath the swing and concentrated on maintaining a gentle, steady rhythm that would soothe the sleeping child. Jenny needed all the breaks she could get. Hayley had been more than willing to watch Rose while Jen had gone into town to meet with one of her few remaining friends. It wasn't easy for the girl to come back to Harrington's Green, Hayley knew. Several of Jenny's former acquaintances had counseled her not to have the child. Others had tried to be supportive after her return, but were ultimately put off by the idea of hanging around with a peer who had a child. Incredibly, Jenny had accepted this lack of understanding with maturity, though not a little sadness. As she reflected now on the woman's famous wild streak, Hayley felt overwhelmed by Jennifer's commitment to love her child despite overwhelming circumstances.

People can *change,* she thought incredulously. *Look at Jenny.*

Her lips curved gently upward in remembrance. *Look at Theadora.*

When the truth about Jenny's whereabouts was first revealed, no one had been more shocked than Hayley. Nothing in her experiences at Newhaven had prepared her for the compassionate side of Theadora Harrington. Yet in retrospect, it all made sense. Carson begging Theadora to step in. Theadora vowing not to lose another Harrington. Jenny running away in shame.

As was the case more often than not, Hayley found herself disagreeing with the manner in which Theadora handled the situation. Carson should have been informed that Jenny was safe. But in her desire to keep control — and to ensure that Jenny did not run even farther and away from her reach — the lady of the manor had remained silent while financially supporting and keeping an eye on the young woman through Theadora's personal secretary, all the while awaiting Jenny's voluntary return, just as she had hoped for the homecoming of her own dear Camilla. It was only after Evan and Simon were charged with theft, briefly detained, and then disappeared into the streets of London that Theadora had proactively encouraged Jenny to return to Newhaven. Thankfully, the young woman was by that time sufficiently homesick and ready to face what she imagined would be her brother's anger.

What Jenny had discovered instead was Carson's love. Gabriel, Hayley, Theadora…each had in his or her own unique way done everything imaginable to make her return a smooth transition. But it was Carson who had met Jenny at the train station and, with tears streaming down his cheeks, reached out to her with a father's arms.

Hayley's eyes grew misty at the thought. Jenny wasn't alone. She, too, relished the feeling of coming home.

In the shade beside her, the tiny bundle began to wriggle and wail. Jenny stirred, tightened her arms protectively around the squirming mass, then stood. "Thanks again, Hayley," she said warmly, her graceful features marked by gratitude.

"My pleasure." Hayley watched as the younger woman crossed the garden, pausing for a moment beside the now-famous sculpture that had become Newhaven's greatest draw. There was no arguing the statue's beauty. No stranger to fine art, Hayley had decided the first time she laid eyes upon it that it was one of the finest pieces she had ever seen. Yet nothing could appear more exquisite to her than the sight of the beautiful young mother standing just beneath it, casting loving eyes upon her treasured child.

Hayley's heart flooded with a wave of thankfulness, as it did so often these days, and she offered up the emotion in silent prayer. This was how she had begun to communicate once more with her God. First by crying out to him with her pain. Later, by asking him for forgiveness — and for help in forgiving others: Theadora, Evan and Simon…even the reverend, who had, to Hayley's dismay, never fully admitted blame, but instead doggedly insisted that he had done the right thing for two young lovers who had needed to escape family manipulation.

For a moment, old instincts kicked in, and Hayley felt herself tense at the memory. Forgiveness, she was finding, was not a one-time affair. Daily, she found herself asking God to help her in her resolve. And slowly, bit by bit, she was learning to let go. Some things were meant to be cherished. Some things were meant to be forgotten.

Hayley's face split into a grin of delight as her most deeply cherished friend and confidante stepped into the clearing. Strolling beneath the shady cover of giant yews, Carson mumbled something that caused bell-like laughter to peal from his sister's lips. Then he took his soft, chubby niece into his long, lanky arms and flashed Hayley a smile rich with pride. Emerald eyes danced.

The moment caught and held.

These were the days worth remembering.

These were the moments she would not forget.

Dear Reader:

Recently, a loved one asked me to describe the type of books I read as a child. Immediately, my thoughts began to race. I thought about the magical stories of C.S. Lewis, Madeleine L'Engle, and Lloyd Alexander. I remembered leafing through the pages of such classics as *Peter Pan* and *Little Women*. I relived countless afternoons spent at the library, listening to the comfortable "thump" as I dropped "just one more" book onto a stack that rivaled my own height.

Wonderfully, I had a brother and friends who shared my passion. As we read, in our minds' eyes we *became* each character. Together, we spent sticky, warm summer afternoons drinking too-sweet Kool-Aid and exploring lands only our minds could see.

For me, reading was more than a hobby; it was life's purest joy. And it still is today.

I'm thankful for the opportunity to share that passion with you. It is my hope that within these pages, you'll find a story that transports you to a place you may never have imagined before. Perhaps it may trigger your own thoughts, questions…even answers that may never before have occurred to you. And as you read, may this story — and others — encourage you to think… inspire you to feel…and draw you somehow closer to the God who never forgets you.

No matter what.

Write to Shari MacDonald
c/o Palisades
P.O.Box 1720
Sisters, Oregon 97759

PALISADES...PURE ROMANCE

THE PALISADES LINE

Refuge, **Lisa Tawn Bergren**
ISBN 0-88070-621-X
Part One: A Montana rancher and a San Francisco marketing exec—only one incredible summer and God could bring such diverse lives together. *Part Two:* Lost and alone, Emily Walker needs and wants a new home, a sense of family. Can one man lead her to the greatest Father she could ever want and a life full of love?

Torchlight, **Lisa Tawn Bergren**
ISBN 0-88070-806-9
When beautiful heiress Julia Rierdon returns to Maine to remodel her family's estate, she finds herself torn between the man she plans to marry and unexpected feelings for a mysterious wanderer who threatens to steal her heart.

Treasure, **Lisa Tawn Bergren**
ISBN 0-88070-725-9
She arrived on the Caribbean island of Robert's Foe armed with a lifelong dream—to find her ancestor's sunken ship—and yet the only man who can help her stands stubbornly in her way. Can Christina and Mitch find their way to the ship *and* to each other?

Cherish, **Constance Colson**
ISBN 0-88070-802-6
Recovering from the heartbreak of a failed engagement, Rose Anson seeks refuge at a resort on Singing Pines Island, where she plans to spend a peaceful summer studying and painting the spectacular scenery of international Lake of the Woods. But when a flamboyant Canadian and a big-hearted American compete for her love, the young artist must face her past—and her future. What follows is a search for the source and meaning of true love: a journey that begins in the heart and concludes in the soul.

Angel Valley, **Peggy Darty**
ISBN 0-88070-778-X
When teacher Laurel Hollingsworth accepts a summer tutoring position for a wealthy socialite family, she faces an enormous challenge in her young student, Anna Lee Wentworth. However, the real challenge is ahead of her: hanging on to her heart when older brother Matthew Wentworth comes to visit. Soon Laurel and Matthew find that they share a faith in God...and powerful feelings for one another. Can Laurel and Matthew find time to explore their relationship while she helps the emotionally troubled Anna Lee and fights to defend her love for the beautiful *Angel Valley?*

Love Song, Sharon Gillenwater
ISBN 0-88070-747-X

When famous country singer Andrea Carson returns to her hometown to recuperate from a life-threatening illness, she seeks nothing more than a respite from the demands of stardom that have sapped her creativity and ability to perform. It's Andi's old high school friend Wade Jamison who helps her to realize that she needs inner healing as well. As Andi's strength grows, so do her feelings for the rancher who has captured her heart. But can their relationship withstand the demands of her career? Or will their romance be as fleeting as a beautiful *Love Song?*

Antiques, Sharon Gillenwater
ISBN 0-88070-801-8

Deeply wounded by the infidelity of his wife, widower Grant Adams swore off all women—until meeting charming antiques dealer Dawn Carson. Although he is drawn to her, Grant struggles to trust again. Dawn finds herself overwhelmingly attracted to the darkly brooding cowboy, but won't marry a non-believer. As Grant learns more about her faith, he is touched by its impact on her life and slowly begins to trust.

Secrets, Robin Jones Gunn
ISBN 0-88070-721-6

Seeking a new life as an English teacher in a peaceful Oregon town, Jessica tries desperately to hide the details of her identity from the community...until she falls in love. Will the past keep Jessica and Kyle apart forever?

Whispers, Robin Jones Gunn
ISBN 0-88070-755-0

Teri Moreno went to Maui eager to rekindle a romance. But when circumstances turn out to be quite different than she expects, she finds herself spending a great deal of time with a handsome, old high school crush who now works at a local resort. But the situation becomes more complicated when Teri meets Gordon, a clumsy, endearing Australian with a wild past, and both men begin to pursue her. Will Teri respond to God's gentle urgings toward true love? The answer lies in her response to the gentle *Whispers* in her heart.

Glory, Marilyn Kok
ISBN 0-88070-754-2

To Mariel Forrest, the teaching position in Taiwan provided more than a simple escape from grief; it also offered an opportunity to deal with her feelings toward the God she once loved, but ultimately blamed for the deaths of her family. Once there, Mariel dares to ask the timeless question: "If God is good, why do we suffer?" What follows is an inspiring story of love, healing, and renewed confidence in God's goodness.

Sierra, **Shari MacDonald**
ISBN 0-88070-726-7
When spirited photographer Celia Randall travels to eastern California for a
short-term assignment, she quickly is drawn to—and locks horns with—editor
Marcus Stratton. Will lingering heartaches destroy Celia's chance at true love? Or
can she find hope and healing high in the *Sierra?*

Westward, **Amanda MacLean**
ISBN 0-88070-751-8
Running from a desperate fate in the South toward an unknown future in the
West, plantation-born artist Juliana St. Clair finds herself torn between two men,
one an undercover agent with a heart of gold, the other a man with evil intentions and a smooth facade. Witness Juliana's dangerous travels toward faith and
love as she follows God's lead in this powerful historical novel.

Stonehaven, **Amanda MacLean**
ISBN 0-88070-757-7
Picking up in the years following *Westward, Stonehaven* follows Callie St. Clair
back to the South where she has returned to reclaim her ancestral home. As she
works to win back the plantation, the beautiful and dauntless Callie turns it into
a station on the Underground Railroad. Covering her actions by playing the role
of a Southern belle, Callie risks losing Hawk, the only man she has ever loved.
Readers will find themselves quickly drawn into this fast-paced novel of treach-
ery, intrigue, spiritual discovery, and unexpected love.

A Christmas Joy, **MacLean, Darty, Gillenwater**
ISBN 0-88070-780-1 (same length as other Palisades books)
Snow falls, hearts change, and love prevails! In this compilation, three experi-
enced Palisades authors spin three separate novelettes centering around the
Christmas season and message:
By Amanda MacLean: A Christmas pageant coordinator in a remote mountain
village of Northern California is reunited with an old friend and discovers the
greatest gift of all.
By Peggy Darty: A college skiclub reunion brings together model Heather Grant
and an old flame. Will they gain a new understanding?
By Sharon Gillenwater: A chance meeting in an airport that neither of them could
forget...and a Christmas reunion.

If you enjoyed reading *Forget-Me-Not*, the following is an excerpt from Shari MacDonald's novel, *Sierra*.

One

~~~

"No untroubled day has ever dawned for me."
Seneca

The sun sank low on the horizon, gracing purple-shadowed foothills with beams of pale spun-gold. One chipped, white diesel pump leaned awkwardly at the side of the highway, a long-abandoned witness to the years of intermittent traffic that had rushed through but rarely paused within the boundaries of Lundy proper.

Behind the wheel of her battered '69 Mustang, Celia yawned and stretched one slim, graceful arm, then the other. "Looks like this is it." She let up on the gas, reluctantly obeying the bright green sign ahead. Though the evening was young, the drive had taken its toll, and her mind held thoughts of little but bath and bed. "What do you say, Hank?" She glanced at the sad-eyed passenger beside her. "Shall we grab a bite before crashing at the new digs?"

At the sound of her voice, the chunky hound tore his eyes from the passing scenery and turned a loving gaze on his owner.

"Now, don't get any big ideas." Celia's voice was stern. "You're on probation, remember? I don't need a repeat of the Memphis chicken incident. But…a dog's got to eat. How about it? Do we need to break out the leash, or can you actually behave yourself?"

Hank blinked at her in adoration, then returned to his vigil at the window.

"Go ahead. Plead the Fifth. See if I care."

Celia wiggled her toes to relieve the cramps brought on by long hours of driving and ran her fingers through her dark, cropped curls. She sighed. The five-day trip from Atlanta had been exhausting. *But Paul would have loved it.* The image of a slim, tanned face and laughing eyes sprung unbidden into her mind. Celia shook her head as if to banish it. Memories were still vivid; it took effort to control them.

"Look!" The sight of a street sign ahead broke Celia's train of thought. "Northeast Hickory. I think that's where the office is located."

Hank obediently looked in the direction she pointed.

"You don't seem too excited. What's the matter? Don't you want to see home base?" Celia quickly turned at the narrow cross street, then fished a scrap of paper out of her purse and checked the address against the buildings they passed.

"Four-two-three…four-two-seven…A-*ha!* Four-two-nine. Bingo! This is it." She pointed to an attractive structure directly across the road, apparently the replica of an old general store. "The home office of *High Sierra* magazine." Celia pulled up in front of an empty ball field and parked behind a mud-spattered Land Cruiser, the only other vehicle in sight. "Let's get a better look. Come on! Give me two minutes, then I promise you dinner fit for a Doberman."

The hound *whoofed* in response and eagerly jumped out of the driver's-side door.

Celia walked across the street toward the office, her admiration growing with each step. It was clear that many of the buildings in Lundy were designed to capture the feel of the Old West. But none she'd seen in passing had appeared as authentic as this one. She climbed three wide stairs to an enormous wooden porch, then paused to examine its great log banisters and pine walls. The beams felt polished and splinterless under her hand, worn smooth from years of wear.

"My goodness! This place is *old*, Furball. I think it's the real thing just spruced up a bit here and there."

The main entrance was only a few feet from where Celia stood. But before she could step toward it, her attention was diverted by the sound of toenails clicking on hardwood as Hank trotted to the end of the porch and disappeared.

"Hey, Magellan," she called. "Wait up!"

Following after her pet, Celia discovered that the porch extended along the left side and around the back of the building. There, she found her hound sitting proudly on top of a weather-stained Adirondak chair, his nose raised high as he sniffed the air repeatedly in assessment of his surroundings.

Smiling at his obvious contentment, Celia turned to survey the view.

"Whew!" She let her breath out slowly. Along the horizon, granite cliffs jutted high against the sky. Frosted by a layer of pure snow, they appeared untouched, unspoiled; kindred spirits standing shoulder to shoulder against the intrusion of man.

"Hello, ladies," Celia whispered up at the powdered peaks. She stood at their feet, feeling small yet strangely significant. After long days of highway noise and radio static, the magnitude of the silence triggered feelings of both shock and relief. Then a door slammed, followed by the close, familiar sound of clicking toenails.

"Stick close to Mom, Hank, " she called over her shoulder. "Okay? Hank?" She turned, but the dog was gone.

"Oh, for crying out loud…Hank?" Celia hurried toward the front of the building, her heart beating faster as a car engine roared to life.

"Hank! HANK!" She leaped down the front steps. Running toward the street, she spied the animal trotting cheerfully in the direction of the Land Cruiser. The driver had already backed up several feet and was now beginning to roll forward into the road.

"Stop! STOP, I SAID!" Celia bounded across both lanes and threw herself against the four-wheel-drive. The vehicle grazed her arm, knocking her off balance as it lurched to a halt.

"Oof!" Celia landed with a thud on something soft, her mind absently registering the sound of a smothered yelp. As she lay on the concrete trying to catch her breath, a tall, athletic-looking man with dark hair and wild eyes jumped out of the vehicle, leaving its door open behind him.

"Are you all right?" He rushed toward her. "I….."

Celia sat up and pointed at the man angrily, her green eyes flashing.

He stopped in his tracks.

"You! You almost killed Hank!" she accused breathlessly. "He was right in front of you, and you almost flattened him!" She sat up gingerly and immediately bent over the animal cowering at her side.

The man looked confused. "But I didn't see anyone…I don't understand how I….." He peered around the front of the Land

Cruiser. "I'm so sorry. Is he all right? Where...?"

Celia gave the tall stranger a look of disgust. "You can't see *anything,* can you? That explains a lot." She turned back to Hank, who wriggled cheerfully under her examination, the fright of the previous moment forgotten.

"What...the *dog?* You threw yourself in front of my truck for a dog? What kind of a crazy person are you? Do you have any idea what you just did? *You're* the one who could have been killed!"

Hank cried out softly as Celia ran her fingers along his tail. "Sorry, bud," she mumbled consolingly. She glared at the man who loomed over her.

"Very nice. First you try to kill my dog. Then you lecture me about living a long life. I'd love to hear more of your valuable advice, but I'm sure you're pretty busy, beating up little old ladies, robbing lemonade stands...or whatever it is you do that's so important you had to rush off without even *looking where you were going.*" Celia scooped Hank up in her arms and stood, drawing herself up to her full five feet four inches of height. She barely reached the man's chin.

The stranger folded his arms and returned her angry look. "Not only are you insane," he said calmly, "you also seem to be hallucinating. If you think I'm the one in the wrong here, I suggest you have your head examined. I may have hit you harder than we realized."

Celia's eyes narrowed to mere slits. "There is nothing wrong with me that your absence won't cure," she said icily. She gave the man one more glare, turned on her heel, and marched back to her car. Upon reaching it, she groaned, realizing the difficulty she would have getting Hank back inside the vehicle. But before she could make a move, the man was beside her, his hand on the passenger door.

"Wait. Look, that came out all wrong. Can we start again here? I really am sorry. But he…Frank, you said? He looks just fine to me. You're the one I'm worried about. For a minute there, I thought.…"

Celia lay the dog gently on the bucket seat and muttered through clenched teeth, "We'll both be fine. If you'll excuse me." She slammed the car door, stalked to the driver's side and climbed in, then sped away without another glance.

The man shook his head and stared as the Mustang became a black speck in the distance. *There goes the most aggravating and beautiful woman I've ever met in my life.*